DAVID HUME

# DAVID HUME

## *Philosopher of Moral Science*

---

## Antony Flew

Basil Blackwell

Copyright © Antony Flew 1986

First published 1986

Basil Blackwell Ltd
108 Cowley Road, Oxford OX4 1JF, UK

Basil Blackwell Inc.
432 Park Avenue South, Suite 1503,
New York, NY 10016, USA

*British Library Cataloguing in Publication Data*
Flew, Antony
  David Hume: philosopher of moral science.
  1. Hume, David, *1711-1776*
  I. Title
  192                        BI498

  ISBN 0-631-13735-1
  ISBN 0-631-15195-8 Pbk

*Library of Congress Cataloging in Publication Data*
Flew, Antony, 1923-
  David Hume, philosopher of moral science.

  Bibliography: p.
  Includes indexes.
  1. Hume, David, 1711-1776.     I. Title.
  B1498.F56   1986     192     86-6826

  ISBN 0-631-13735-1
  ISBN 0-631-15195-8 (pbk.)

Typeset by DMB (Typesetting), Oxford
Printed in Great Britain by Page Bros., Norwich

For those many students who
in all the years of a long
teaching life have joined with
me in respectful, affectionate
yet always critical study of the
philosophical writings of 'le
bon David'.

# Contents

# Abbreviations

The following abbreviations are used in references made in parentheses to Hume's works. Short titles are used in the text.

DNR – *Dialogues concerning Natural Religion* (1779)

EHU – *An Enquiry concerning Human Understanding* (1748) (referred to in the text as the first *Enquiry*)

EPM – *An Enquiry concerning the Principles of Morals* (1751) (referred to in the text as the second *Enquiry*)

NHR – *The Natural History of Religion* (1757)

THN – *A Treatise of Human Nature* (1739-40) (referred to in the text as the *Treatise*)

# 1

## What is to be Done

In the Preface to a recent book on *Hume's Skepticism* the author takes note of, and welcomes, "the robust state of Hume scholarship". He then remarks that this "raises a question . . . The question, of course, is why another book on Hume, in particular, why another *general* book on Hume?" (Fogelin, 1985, p. xi). Certainly many further and often excellent works have appeared since the first publication in 1941 of Norman Kemp Smith's revolutionary survey, *The Philosophy of David Hume*. It is, however, not obvious that the rising tide of attention has been disproportionate to the importance of its subject. In the present case there are also more particular answers.

First: several of the more general books have been potboilers, written simply to fill a Hume-shaped gap in some series. Usually these fillers are not sufficiently wide-ranging to constitute really satisfactory introductions. For instance, in one the author states: both, that "In this book I am trying to provide a comprehensive interpretation of Hume's philosophy . . ."; and, that "I have tried throughout to make what I say intelligible to beginners, or virtual beginners in philosophy, while also providing something of interest to Hume scholars and to philosophers dealing with the problems he discussed" (Stroud, 1977, pp. ix and x). But in the paragraph immediately following the first of these two claims the same author goes on to announce that he will be making no attempt to tackle: either Hume's philosophy of religion; or the philosophical aspect of Hume's work in history and in political economy.

To observe these restrictions may or may not be required by concentration upon "the most fundamental parts of Hume's philosophy" (Stroud, 1977, p. ix). But certainly it is bound to deprive those "beginners, or virtual beginners" of much which they should find im-

mediately exciting. It also introduces grave distortions into their picture of Hume. For there is no doubt but that he himself set great store
by some of the materials thus ignored, believing them to include
valuable findings: his elegant counter to the traditional Argument to
Design, for instance; and Hume's Check, his demonstration that
there can never be historical evidence adequate to warrant the belief
that a miracle occurred – or, at any rate, not "so as to be the foundation of a system of religion". Although the present book still cannot be
completely comprehensive the topics selected for either comparative
or total neglect are those in which Hume was not at his best, or those
about which few of our contemporaries are able to raise much interest.

Second: although this is a book about Hume's philosophy only, it
will treat that in the perspective of all his contributions to what in his
day were called moral subjects. That last expression is roughly equivalent to 'human studies'. It covers not only history and the other
social sciences but also psychology. Hume's contributions were in fact
substantial. Indeed he has to be rated, along with his younger friends
Adam Ferguson and Adam Smith, among the Scottish Founding
Fathers of social science (Hayek, 1967, chs. 6 and 7).

Significantly, his very first publication, in three books, was *A
Treatise of Human Nature* – hereinafter referred to either as THN or as
the *Treatise*. Even more significantly its subtitle was "An ATTEMPT
to introduce the experimental Method of Reasoning into MORAL
SUBJECTS"; although, by arguing in his Introduction that there can
be no valid experimentation in introspective psychology, he showed
that the word should have been not 'experimental' but 'experiential'.
It is scarcely surprising that, at a time when physics was known everywhere as natural philosophy, Hume made no sharp and consistent
distinction: between, on the one hand, his contributions to psychology
and, on the other hand, what we should today admit as his pure philosophy. Nevertheless, while insisting upon the modern distinction,
our intention here is to present that philosophy in such a way as to
reveal both its connections and its lacks of connection with what
we shall, conservatively and piously, continue to categorize as the
moral sciences.

Third: no previous study of Hume's philosophy has made nearly
enough of the fact that almost all his conclusions are, for better or for
worse, conditioned and sometimes determined by an interlocking set
of Cartesian assumptions. These he continues always to accept with-

out question as "the obvious dictates of reason", which "no man who reflects ever doubted". Given these assumptions extreme scepticism becomes inescapable. In consequence it certainly would have been true to say, in the antediluvian epoch before Kemp Smith, what recently has been said, but falsely, of our own time: namely, that "David Hume is generally considered to be a purely negative philosopher – the arch sceptic whose primary aim and achievement was to reduce the theories of his empiricist predecessors to the absurdity which was implicitly contained in them all along" (Stroud, 1977, p. 1).

Yet even in those now far off days no one seems to have emphasized that Hume's initial assumptions consisted in a close-connected set, a set offered as interim conclusions by Descartes in the first two paragraphs of Part IV of *A Discourse on the Method*. Not having made enough of this at the beginning, and rarely recognizing how grotesquely paradoxical the whole set is, earlier interpreters have failed to point the strangeness, the often self-frustrating perversity, of some of the positions which Hume was misled to adopt later.

Consider, for example, two consequences of accepting what should be seen as a most bizarre contention, that people are essentially incorporeal. Descartes, notoriously, came to this through meditating alone in a room with a stove: "And then, examining attentively that which I was, I saw that I could conceive that I had no body, and that there was no world nor place where I might be; but yet that I could not for all that conceive that I was not . . . From that I knew that I was a substance the whole essence or nature of which is to think, and for its existence there is no need of any place, nor does it depend on any material thing; so that this 'me', that is to say, the soul by which I am what I am, is entirely distinct from body, and is even more easy to know than is the latter; and even if body were not, the soul would not cease to be what it is" (Descartes, 1637, I, p. 101).

For predecessors like Locke and Berkeley, hoping to justify immortalist conclusions, it was easy and natural to agree. But Hume was eventually going to defend a contrary, mortalist position. So it is remarkable, and should always have been remarked, that Hume does not think to protest: either that 'person' and all other person-words are, and have to be, taught as words for members of a certain very special sort of creatures of flesh and blood; or that minds and 'selves' can be identified only as the minds or 'selves' of the particular creatures of flesh and blood whose minds or 'selves' they are.

Instead Hume is, it appears, entirely happy to grant, from the beginning of his discussion 'Of personal identity', that a "self or person" is (not an incorporeal substance but) "nothing but a bundle or collection of different perceptions, which succeed each other with an inconceivable rapidity, and are in a perpetual flux and movement" (THN I (iv) 6, pp. 251 and 252). The ungullible Hume – as Gilbert Ryle loved to call him – thus challenges not the incorporeality but the substantiality of the "self or person"; while without question taking the last two terms to be straightforwardly synonymous.

Again, in searching for the experiential source 'Of the idea of necessary connexion' Hume thinks always and only of such tightly limited experience as might possibly be enjoyed by a bodiless observer; never of that which, as corporeal agents acting upon other corporeal objects, all of us persons do actually have.

Thus, considering as "resembling instances" cases in which events of one particular sort are closely and regularly followed by events of another particular sort, Hume says: "Tho' the several resembling instances, which give rise to the idea of power, have no influence on each other, and can never produce any new quality *in the object*, which can be the model of that idea, yet the observation of this resemblance produces a new impression in *the mind*, which is its real model. For, after we have *observ'd* the resemblance in a sufficient number of instances, we immediately feel a determination of the mind to pass from one object to its immediate attendant . . . These instances are in themselves totally distinct from each other, and have no union but in the mind, which *observes* them, . . . Necessity, then, is the effect of this *observation* . . ." (THN I (iii) 14, pp. 164-5: the last three sets of italics supplied). Concluding, therefore, that any idea, or perhaps only any seeming idea, of power or necessity or impossibility must be "*in the mind*" rather than "*in the object*" Hume is confident that there are and can be no objective physical necessities or objective physical impossibilities either experienced or experiencable in the Universe around us.

This carries several embarrassing consequences. From time to time some of these have been noticed. But they have rarely, if ever, been tracked down to their source in the Cartesian assumption of personal incorporeality. For instance, in *An Enquiry concerning Human Understanding* – hereinafter referred to either as EHU or as the first *Enquiry* – Hume, having completed his proposed reconciliation 'Of Liberty and

Necessity', goes on: first, to suggest that it is not possible "to explain distinctly, how the Deity can be the mediate cause of all the actions of men, without being the author of sin and moral turpitude"; and then to draw the congenial, aggressively agnostic moral that "mere natural and unassisted reason is very unfit to handle" such mysteries, and hence that she should, "leaving a scene so full of obscurities and perplexities, return, with suitable modesty, to her true and proper province, the examination of common life" (EHU VII (ii), p. 103).

But this will not do. For Hume's Compatibilist reconciliation 'Of Liberty and Necessity' can go through only "by giving a new definition of necessity" (Hume, 1740, p. 661); a definition which reduced physical necessity to a mere regularity of succession. Yet, if that were all there was to the necessity of causes, then neither God, nor man, could be the Author, or authors, "of sin and moral turpitude"; or, indeed, of anything else. For there would in such a world be no such thing as bringing anything about; making it physically necessary for that something to happen, and physically impossible for it not to (Flew, 1978b).

Again, in his methodological argument about evidence for the occurrence of miracles, Hume contends: "But in order to encrease the probability against the testimony of witnesses, let us suppose, that the fact, which they affirm, instead of being only marvellous, is really miraculous . . ." (EHU X (i), p. 114). If there really is no such thing as either physical necessity or its opposite, physical impossibility, then this crucial distinction must collapse. So, although he may still be entitled to employ it in an ad hominem argument against someone refusing to adopt his own reductionist account of physical necessity and physical impossibility, Hume has no business to suggest that it could, on his own principles, make sense to describe some conceivable occurrence not merely as marvellous but, additionally, as genuinely miraculous; and hence, as such, physically impossible. Furthermore, by the same token, Hume disqualifies himself from appealing, in his future work as an historian, to any knowledge of anything supposed to be physically necessary or physically impossible. This would be a catastrophic disqualification; which, of course, as a practising historian Hume felt no shame about ignoring totally.

The brief indications given above of the three main ways in which the present book differs from its predecessors should be a sufficient answer to Fogelin's fair question. The next tasks are: to give an account of Hume's life and works; and to review the whole constellation of Cartesian assumptions constituting the starting point of Hume's philosophy. Both of these exercises are necessary propaedeutics for anyone hoping to achieve a sufficient sympathetic understanding.

## 1 HUME'S LIFE AND WORKS

He was born in Edinburgh in 1711. His family was well-connected on both sides, though its estate at Ninewells in Berwickshire was small. In our own time the same extended family has supplied a Prime Minister. But the kinship claims of the notorious nineteenth-century physical medium D. D. Home were, it seems, as bogus as the rest of his performances (Hall, 1984, ch. 1). Hume's father died in 1713, leaving three children to their mother, "a woman of singular merit, who, though young and handsome, devoted herself entirely to the rearing and education of her children". In 1723, a few weeks before his twelfth birthday, David was admitted to Edinburgh University along with his elder brother John. He left, without taking a degree, in 1725 or 1726. The next few years were spent studying at home: "My studious disposition, my sobriety, and my industry gave my family a notion that the law was a proper profession for me. But I found an insurmountable aversion to everything but the pursuits of philosophy and general learning, and while they fancied I was poring over Voet and Vinnius, Cicero and Vergil were the authors which I was secretly devouring."

In 1734, after a certain Anne Galbraith had accused him of fathering her third child conceived out of wedlock, Hume entered the office of a West Indies merchant in Bristol. This venture was brief and half-hearted. He withdrew to France: "During my retreat in France, first at Rheims, but chiefly at La Flèche, in Anjou, I composed my *Treatise of Human Nature.*" At La Flèche he had contacts with the famous Jesuit college which had educated Descartes. In 1737 he returned to London, to arrange publication. But even before the first two books appeared, early in 1739, he had returned to Ninewells.

Book III followed in 1740. But earlier in that year Hume published *An Abstract of a Treatise of Human Nature* – hereinafter referred to as the *Abstract*, and as reprinted in the standard Clarendon edition of the *Treatise*. This *Abstract*, like the *Treatise* itself, was anonymous, and commended the author in the third person. It was only in the late thirties of the present century that the Cambridge economists J. M.

Keynes and P. Sraffa proved that it must have been written by Hume. It is no more than a pamphlet, but significant as revealing what, at that time, he believed were his most important contributions: "Thro' this whole book, there are great pretensions to new discoveries in philosophy; but if anything can intitle the author to so glorious a name as that of an *inventor*, 'tis the use he makes of the principle of the association of ideas, which enters into most of his philosophy" (pp. 661-2).

The particular "philosophy" into which this principle enters so generously is what we should see as Hume's attempt at a paramechanical science of psychology. Familiar from his reading of Descartes with the metaphysical dichotomy of mind and matter, conceived as consciousness and stuff, and believing that the classical mechanics of Newton constituted a definitive science of the latter, Hume saw an opening for a new science of the former, in which ideas as moments of consciousness would parallel Newton's "hard, massy and impenetrable" atoms, and the principles of association the fundamental mechanical forces.

Hume was, like so many a young author both before and since, disappointed with the reception of his first book. In the brief notes on *My Own Life*, from which all the autobiographical quotations in the present section 1 are drawn, and which he composed during one of the last months of his life, Hume wrote words which have consoled many an equally, if more deservedly, disappointed successor: "Never literary attempt was more unfortunate than my *Treatise of Human Nature*. It fell deadborn from the press, without reaching such distinction as even to excite a murmer among the zealots."

Next, in 1742, the first fifteen *Essays, Moral and Political* appeared in Edinburgh, again anonymously. They were successful. Other editions and more essays followed. These were the first of Hume's works to bear his name. Urbane and sometimes slight they are relevant to us mainly as indications of Hume's lifelong, consistent concern for human studies. "In these four sciences of *Logic, Morals, Criticism, and Politics*," he had written in the Introduction to the *Treatise*, "is comprehended almost everything which it can any way import us to be acquainted with, or which can tend either to the improvement or ornament of the human mind" (pp. xix-xx). All references will be given in the page numbers of the now standard Liberty Press edition, which collects all *The Essays of David Hume* including those which were for various reasons suppressed during his lifetime.

In 1745 the electors to the Professorship of Ethics and Pneumatical Philosophy in Edinburgh preferred the otherwise unmemorable William Cleghorn to a man whom "the zealots" had already identified as a "notorious infidel". In the same year Hume accepted the job of tutor to the young Marquess of Annandale, who turned out to be certifiably insane. In 1746 Hume served as secretary to General St. Clair in an abortive raid on the coast of France, and in 1747 accompanied him on a military embassy to the courts of Vienna and Turin.

The next major literary event in Hume's life was the appearance in 1748 of the *Philosophical Essays concerning Human Understanding*, to which Hume in 1758 gave their present title, *An Enquiry concerning Human Understanding*. In the autobiography he states: "I had always entertained a notion that my want of success in publishing the *Treatise of Human Nature* had proceeded more from the manner than the matter, and that I had been guilty of a very usual indiscretion in going to the press too early. I therefore cast the first part of that work anew in the *Enquiry concerning Human Understanding* . . ."

The result, however, is not just a better written and better arranged second edition of Book I of the *Treatise*. Certainly where the first *Enquiry* covers the same ground this description does apply. But the whole is much shorter, and several of the topics previously discussed at some length are either omitted altogther or treated only sketchily and by the way. On the other hand, of the twelve sections into which this *Enquiry* is divided, two were not anticipated at all in the *Treatise* as published. The qualification of those last two words is important. For in a letter to his advocate friend Henry Home, the future Lord Kames, written while preparing his manuscript for the press, Hume wrote: "I am at present castrating my work, that is, cutting off its nobler parts; that is, endeavouring it shall give as little offence as possible, before which I could not pretend to put it in the Doctor's hands" (Greig, 1932, I, p. 25).

Enclosed with this letter were "some *Reasonings concerning Miracles*, which I once thought of publishing with the rest, but which I am afraid will give too much offence, even as the world is disposed at present" (ibid., p. 24). Obviously these became a draft for section X 'Of Miracles'. Presumably a draft of section XI and perhaps of the essay 'Of the Immortality of the Soul' were also among those "nobler parts" which, with discreet brutality, Hume was engaged in excising.

Certainly the first two of these together constitute most of the polemic point of the later work; while, equally certainly, they were among the "improvements . . . in natural religion" which the Introduction to the earlier had promised, "were we [to become] thoroughly acquainted with the extent and force of human understanding". We should therefore, Hume had urged there, "leave the tedious lingring method, which we have hitherto followed, and instead of taking now and then a castle or village on the frontier, . . . march up directly to the capital . . . to human nature itself" (*THN*, pp. xix and xx).

Together these additions, or restorations, sustain the agnostic yet aggressive main morals of the first *Enquiry*: that the question of the nature of God lies outwith the scope of our understandings; and that we ought, therefore, to concentrate our investigative efforts upon this world, and its affairs (their "true and proper province, the examination of common life"). The Doctor whose high opinion Hume was keen to win was Dr Joseph Butler, eventually to be appointed Bishop of Durham. Since, in that century, a commitment of Christian faith was a prerequisite for such appointments, Hume might have discounted any unfavourable verdict by putting the Bishop down as one of "the zealots". But in fact Hume abandoned the project of approaching Butler upon hearing of his earlier elevation to the see of Bristol.

In 1749, following the publication of the first *Enquiry*, Hume returned to Ninewells, but removed to Edinburgh in 1751. In that same year Glasgow preferred the otherwise unknown James Clow to Hume for its Professor of Logic. (What, nevertheless, is truly remarkable about Hume's two attempts to secure an academic appointment, and very much to Scotland's credit, is not that they were eventually unsuccessful but that they ever came near to succeeding. For where else, in those days, would the application of a man reputed to be an infidel have been so long considered?) Late in 1751 or early in 1752 comes *An Enquiry concerning the Principles of Morals*, "which is another part of my *Treatise* that I cast anew." This will always be referred to as either the second *Enquiry* or EPM. It covers afresh the ground of Book III 'Of Morals'. But here there is no question but that there has been some development as well as very drastic revision and rewriting.

Next, and certainly in 1752, came the *Political Discourses*. This was "the only work of mine that was successful on the first publication". These are much more substantial and important than the *Essays,*

*Moral and Political*. They had considerable influence on some of the Founding Fathers of the United States of America. (Incidentally, Hume himself early formed and consistently maintained a strong sympathy with the national aspirations of the American colonists.) These *Political Discourses* include several historically important contributions to political economy. Along with relevant extracts from his correspondence with Montesquieu, Turgot and Smith these have been collected as *David Hume: Writings on Economics* (Rotwein, 1953). The *Political Discourses* themselves are, of course, all included in the Liberty Press edition of the *Essays*.

In 1752 Hume became Librarian to the Faculty of Advocates in Edinburgh, and was thus able to start work on what eventually became his *History of England, from the Invasion of Julius Caesar to the Revolution in 1688*. But since – as the wittily cross-grained Earl Monboddo was to say – Hume wrote history "as witches used to say their prayers – backwards" the first volume to be published, in 1754, was on the Stuarts. So it was with the volume starting with Caesar's invasion that the whole project was completed in 1762. Years later, when his publisher offered a very generous contract in order to induce Hume to add a final volume covering the period from the Glorious Revolution up to the present his response is said to have been, as always, courteous; yet at the same time memorably decisive: "I must decline not only this offer, but all others of a literary nature for four reasons: Because I am too old, too fat, too lazy and too rich" (Mossner, 1954, pp. 555-6).

This *History of England* quickly became and, until it was replaced by Macaulay, long remained, both a standard work and a best-seller. The Catalogue of the British Library still lists the author as "Hume, David, the historian". His work was commended by Voltaire for its truly scientific detachment: "Mr Hume, in his *History*, is neither parliamentarian, nor royalist, nor Anglican, nor Presbyterian – he is simply judicial . . . we find a mind superior to his materials; he speaks of weaknesses, blunders, cruelties as a physician speaks of epidemic diseases" (Voltaire, 1883-7 vol. XXV, pp. 169-73). The verdict, however, has not been unanimous. Thomas Jefferson, though famously dedicated to the absolute freedom of the human mind, had an offending copy removed from the library of his University of Virginia: "it is this book which has undermined free principles of the English government . . . and has spread universal toryism over the land" (Quoted in Livingston, 1984, p. 264; and compare both Bongie, 1965 and Okie, 1985).

The modest fortune which Hume progressively accumulated was derived partly from royalties on his publications and partly from the emoluments of various official employments. By 1761 his literary reputation was sufficient for all his works to be admitted to the *Index Librorum prohibitorum* in Rome. In 1763 the Earl of Hertford asked him to serve as his secretary on an embassy in Paris. This was an inspired choice, for Hume was immediately lionized in all the society salons. He even did the formal side of the job well enough to be left for a time as chargé d'affaires. In 1766 he returned from France with Jean-Jacques Rousseau in tow. Hume made great efforts to arrange an acceptable retreat for his protégé in England. The ever impossible Rousseau repaid every kindness with suspicion, animosity and abuse. In 1767 Hume accepted the important Undersecretaryship of the Northern Department of the Secretary of State in London. This post he resigned in 1769, in order to retire finally to Edinburgh.

There he lived, and was loved, as the doyen of the Scottish Enlightenment. But in 1775 he was struck by a fatal wasting disease of the bowels. Unshaken in his assurance of annihilation, continuing to receive friends as affably as always, and to send corrections of his works to the printers, he followed faithfully the family motto: "True to the end". He died in 1776, the year of the American Declaration of Independence, something which he had anticipated, and welcomed, in 1775: "I am an American in my principles, and wish we would let them alone to govern or misgovern themselves as they think proper" (Mossner, 1954, p. 554).

Earlier in the same fatal year Hume had thanked the still unfamous Edward Gibbon for the gift of copies of the first volumes of *The Decline and Fall of the Roman Empire* in terms which – as the delighted Gibbon said – "overpaid the labour of ten years" (ibid., p. 229). Hume read too, and congratulated his friend Adam Smith upon, that first and greatest masterpiece of development economics: *An Inquiry into the Nature and Causes of the Wealth of Nations*. He also sent to his publishers an Advertisement which was to be, and was, prefixed to a new edition of *Essays and Treatises on Several Subjects*; two volumes containing all those of his works, other than the *History* and the *Dialogues*, which he wished preserved. This Advertisement categorically repudiated the *Treatise*. Those who "direct all their batteries against that juvenile work, which the Author never acknowledged", display "a bigotted zeal", giving rise to "a practice very contrary to all the rules of candour and fair-dealing".

But the main literary business of his last months was preparing his *Dialogues concerning Natural Religion* for the press, and ensuring that they would in fact be published after his death. These *Dialogues*, also cited as DNR, Hume had begun at least as early as 1751. But his own caution and the pressure of his friends prevented him from publishing them in his own lifetime. The whole story is pieced together in Kemp Smith's definitive edition; an edition which also established the more disputatious conclusion that, in so far as any character speaks for Hume himself, as certainly no one character always does, it has to be Philo (DNR, App. C and Introduction; compare Gaskin, 1978, passim).

The *Dialogues* complement the first of *Four Dissertations*, first published in 1757. That, *The Natural History of Religion*, also cited as NHR, is an essay on the origin and development of religion, considered as a natural phenomenon. It seeks the causes of this development and the motivating reasons for belief; and is, therefore, a contribution to the sociology of religion. The *Dialogues*, on the other hand, look for and discuss evidencing reasons. This distinction between evidencing and motivating reasons is, perhaps, most relevantly made by reference to Pascal's Wager. For, whereas all the other standard arguments of Natural Theology offered what are supposed to be evidences, suggesting that certain commended propositions are true, that urged – notwithstanding that (evidencing) "Reason can decide nothing here" – that we should be madly imprudent not to labour to persuade ourselves into the Faith (Flew, 1971, ch. VI 7). So, from the "juvenile" *Treatise* to the posthumous *Dialogues*, Hume's philosophy is always connected with, if not always so carefully distinguished from, his contributions to the moral sciences.

## 2 THE INTERLOCKING CARTESIAN ASSUMPTIONS

At the beginning of Part IV of the *Discourse*, after a smoothly discursive buildup in the three suave and apparently innocuous Parts I-III, Descartes suddenly releases a shattering salvo of almost all-destroying doubt. Just as Goethe, who was present, said that the cannonade of

Valmy opened a new era in human history, so, with equal truth, it can be asserted that the modern period in philosophy starts with this single devastating sentence: "Thus, because our senses sometimes deceive us, I wished to suppose that nothing is just as they cause us to imagine it to be, and because there are men who deceive themselves in their reasoning, and fall into paralogisms, . . . judging that I was as subject to error as any other, I rejected as false all the reasons formerly accepted by me as demonstrations" (p. 101).

So, because (? we know that) we are sometimes mistaken in our judgements about the furniture of the Universe around us, and conceivably always might be, perhaps we never really know anything about what is there the case; and because (?we know that) we have sometimes been mistaken about the validity of inferences, and conceivably always might be, perhaps we can never truly identify any argument as valid or any demonstration as genuine. Next Descartes proceeds to pick out what alone seems to remain of rock-solid certainty: "But immediately afterwards I noticed that whilst I thus wished to think all things false, it was absolutely essential that the 'I' who thought this should be somewhat . . ." Hence "this truth, '*I think therefore I am*'" became "so certain and so assured that all the most extravagant suppositions brought forward by the sceptics were incapable of shaking it . . ." (p. 101).

It is important to recognize that for Descartes the word 'thought' has, officially, a much wider than usual signification. It covers, not only the activity in which Rodin's *Le Penseur* is engaged, but also the enjoying or not enjoying of any and every form of consciousness – including the suffering of pains which may make ratiocination impossible. This comes out most clearly in a later work, *The Principles of Philosophy*. There, in Principle IX of Part I, Descartes writes: "By the word 'thought' I understand all that of which we are conscious as operating in us. And that is why not alone understanding, willing, imagining, but also feeling, are here the same thing as thought. For if I say I see, or I walk, I therefore am, and if by seeing and walking I mean the action of my eyes or my legs, which is the work of my body, my conclusion is not absolutely certain; because it may be that, as often happens in sleep, I think I see or I walk, although I never open my eyes or move from my place, and the same thing perhaps might occur if I had not a body at all" (p. 222).

In thus identifying thought, and hence the mind, with con-
ciousness, Descartes was in effect introducing a fresh criterion of the
mental. Successors who had accepted this criterion were, therefore,
entirely right to dismiss all talk of the unconscious mind as, in their
own understanding, flat self-contradictory. Where, of course, they
were wrong was in not appreciating that colleagues talking in  this
way were employing a different criterion, which they wished to
recommend as heuristically more fertile. More immediately relevant,
the introduction of this fresh criterion: first posed the problem of providing some account of the relations or lack of relations between the
two radically different worlds of stuff and of consciousness; and then,
after Newton, suggested that there might be room for what Hume was
to attempt to construct – a kind of para-mechanics of the latter.

Having discovered that "this truth, '*I think therefore I am*'" was "so
certain and so assured that all the most extravagant suppositions
brought forward by the sceptics were incapable of shaking it . . .", the
next step was that of "examining attentively that which I was . . ."
Descartes here begins not from what he believes that he has just
established – the inexpugnable certainty of present consciousness –
but from what he thinks he can or cannot conceive – what, that is, it
would not or would be self-contradictory or otherwise incoherent to
say. "I saw," he goes on, "that I could conceive that I had no body,
and that there was no world or place where I might be; but yet that I
could not for all that conclude that I was not." From these premises
he derives the conclusion quoted in the previous section 1: "From that
I knew that I was a substance the whole essence or nature of which is
to think, that for its existence there is no need of any place, nor does it
depend on any material thing; so that this 'me', that is to say, the soul
by which I am what I am, is entirely distinct from body . . .; and even
if body were not, the soul would not cease to be what it is" (p. 101).

We are now in a position to distinguish three main elements in this
so seductively presented Cartesian vision. All three are assumptions
which Hume took to be "the obvious dictates of reason", which "no
man, who reflects, ever doubted"; although it was to only one of them
that he directed these explicit words (EHU XII (i), p. 152). First, in
the order of appearance in Descartes, comes the complex idea that
knowledge is possible only where it is inconceivable that there might
be error, and that no knowledge claim can be adequately vindicated
by offering any evidencing reason for belief which does not actually

entail the truth of the proposition asserted as known. Although this principle, or these principles, are rarely, if ever, both formulated clearly and boldly proclaimed, it has, or they have, continued to guide or to misguide philosophers, and not philosophers only, ever since Descartes tacitly appealed to it, or to them, in that first paragraph of Part IV of the *Discourse*.

It should by now be easy to see that this is indeed the appeal which was being made. Let us waive what is for us at the moment a peripheral objection; that Descartes appears to be appealing to knowledge of the detection of previous mistakes in order to support the supposition that knowledge is, in the areas of these mistakes, altogether impossible. For there is no question but that the Cartesian case for extreme scepticism does depend upon the first assumption aforementioned. Consider, for instance, the way in which this case was put in the *Principles*, in the course of defining the word 'thought'. "Because it may be that, as often happens in sleep, I think I see or I walk, although I never open my eyes or move from my place", no conclusion in any way based upon such sensory experience is "absolutely certain" or, what presumably amounts to the same thing, truly known. Yet the only reason, or reasons, either offered or available for maintaining such scepticism is, or are, that error is here conceivable, and that the statement that it seemed to people that they perceived something does not entail that they actually did.

The second assumption is, as we have just seen, derived from the first. In resolving "to assume that everything that ever entered into my mind was no more true than the illusions of my dreams" Descartes was proposing to take it that we are never immediately and non-inferentially aware of anything outside and independent of ourselves. We are instead immediately and non-inferentially aware only of successive moments of our logically private consciousness. To employ more picturesque language: we are each and all of us separately and individually shut off from any External World which may or may not exist; and which is in any case necessarily and for ever hidden behind an impenetrable Veil of Appearance.

The third assumption, as we have already seen in section 1, is that persons are essentially incorporeal. Although Descartes also offers an argument proceeding from premises stating what he believes to be or not to be conceivable, this third assumption can be derived from the first and second much as the second so obviously is in its turn derived from the first. The nub of the matter is that the answer to Gilbert Ryle's question, 'What is the External World external to?' has to begin with an equally Rylean phrase, 'The Ghost in the Machine'. For in Cartesian terms all bodies, including human bodies, must be elements in the External World. Or – if a more epistemological formulation is preferred – if we are indeed for ever confined to an immediate awareness only of our own logically private consciousness, and if statements about that private consciousness can never possess sufficient logical strength to entail any conclusions about a mind-independent public world, then none of us can ever know that he or she possesses, or is, a body.

It is perhaps just worth pointing out that the final phrase in the previous paragraph carries false suggestions. For an incorporeal something could not have a sex; or, in the fashionable perverse misusage, a gender. (To the extent that gender, in the grammarian's traditional sense, is not necessarily related to sex, an incorporeal person perhaps could have a gender!) It is, however, more relevant to our present purposes to round off chapter 1 with quotations showing that at least the second of these three Cartesian assumptions, and therefore the third, were also accepted by both Locke and Berkeley, Hume's chief immediate British predecessors.

In Locke the 'thoughts' of Descartes become 'ideas', and it is not without reason that at the beginning of *An Essay concerning Human Understanding* he apologizes to the reader "for the frequent use of the Word *Idea*, which he will find in the following Treatise. It being that Term, which, I think, serves best to stand for whatsoever is the Object of the Understanding when a Man thinks, I have used it to express whatever is meant by *Phantasm, Notion, Species,* or whatever it is, which the Mind can be employed about in thinking . . ." (I (i) 8, p. 47).

Berkeley too follows the same "new way of ideas". For the opening sentence of *The Principles of Human Knowledge* reads: "It is evident to anyone who takes a survey of the *objects of human knowledge*, that they are either *ideas* actually imprinted on the senses; or else such as are perceived by attending to the passions and operations of the mind; or, lastly, *ideas* formed by help of memory and imagination – either compounding, dividing, or barely representing those originally perceived in the aforesaid ways." On the contrary: it is not evident at all. It is, rather, "the bottom, one might perhaps call it, of the garden path"; the garden path up which that most brilliant of Irishmen will so gently and so genially lead us into the fairyland of philosophical idealism (Austin, 1962a, p. 6).

Since the three interlocking Cartesian assumptions that we have been distinguishing are never clearly and distinctly formulated as fundamental guiding principles either by Descartes himself or by Hume, it may be helpful to conclude this chapter with a brief restatement. First comes the assumption that all arguments must be either deductive or defective, since the only sufficient reasons for believing any proposition are (other) propositions which entail it. Second is the notion that we are (all of us) forever imprisoned behind Veils of Appearance, since we can never be immediately aware of any mind-independent realities. Third, and finally, it is argued or assumed that we essentially are incorporeal subjects of (only) the limited and ingrown sort of experience allowed for under the second of these three principles.

# 2

# Impressions, Ideas and the External World

Both the *Treatise* and the first *Enquiry* are projects in the same genre as that of Locke's *Essay concerning Human Understanding*. These in their turn were eventually to stimulate Immanuel Kant to write his three great *Critiques*. "I freely admit," he confessed in the Preface of *Prolegomena to any Future Metaphysics that will be able to present itself as Science*, "it was David Hume's remark that first, many years ago, interrupted my dogmatic slumber and gave a completely different direction to my enquiries in the field of speculative philosophy" (Kant, 1783, p. 9). All these works can and should be seen as items in a continuing tradition. In our own time that tradition also embraces Wittgenstein's *Tractatus Logico-Philosophicus*. For although its author might have been reluctant to acknowledge this ancestry, his conclusions reveal a fundamental similarity of intentions: "To say nothing except what can be said, i.e. the propositions of natural science . . . This . . . would be the only strictly correct method . . . Whereof one cannot speak, thereof one must be silent" (Wittgenstein, 1921, p. 189; and compare Jones, 1976).

In a prefatory Epistle to the Reader Locke had explained both how he came to undertake his project and what he hoped to achieve: ". . . five or six Friends meeting at my Chamber, and discoursing upon a Subject very remote from this, found themselves quickly at a stand, by the Difficulties that rose on every side. After we had a while puzzled our selves, without coming any nearer a Resolution of those Doubts which perplexed us, it came into my Thoughts, that we took a wrong course; and that, before we set our selves upon Enquiries of that Nature, it was necessary to examine our own Abilities, and see, what Objects our Understandings were, or were not fitted to deal with" (p. 7). There is evidence to suggest that the very remote subject about

which these friends "found themselves quickly at a stand" was of exactly that kind which Hume was to contend that "our Understandings
. . . were not fitted to deal with".

## 1 PSYCHOLOGICAL AND ETYMOLOGICAL EMPIRICISM

In *Treatise, Abstract*, and first *Enquiry* Hume begins the main business
by proclaiming his (psychological) empiricist principle. "The first
proposition", as he puts it in the *Abstract*, "is that all our ideas, or
weak perceptions, are derived from our impressions, or strong
perceptions; and that we can never think of anything we have not seen
without us or felt in our own minds" (p. 647). This, Hume suggests,
is an improved version of what Locke was after in denying the existence of innate ideas. One part of the improvement claimed consists
in subdividing the extremely comprehensive category of Lockean
ideas. These are, as near as makes no matter, the referents of the term
'thoughts', as redefined by Descartes. These Hume now relabels
"perceptions of the human mind", sorting them into two fundamentally
different kinds, impressions and ideas: "The difference betwixt these
consists in the degrees of force and liveliness, with which they strike
upon the mind, and make their way into our thought and consciousness." Impressions comprise "all our sensations, passions and
emotions, as they make their first appearance in the soul". Ideas are
"the faint images of these in thinking and reasoning . . ." (THN I (i)
1, p. 1). Both impressions and ideas may be either simple or complex.
   The next step is to argue that "all our ideas or more feeble perceptions are copies of our impressions or more lively ones" (EHU II,
p. 19). This contention replaces Locke's denial of innate ideas, a
denial to which he had devoted the whole of Book I of his *Essay*. Hume
now is ready to deploy a systematic challenge. Reverting to everyday
interpretations of the two key terms, in which ideas are a kind of con-
stituents of thoughts, he urges: "When we entertain, therefore, any
suspicion that a philosophical term is employed without any meaning
or idea (as is but too frequent), we need but enquire, *from what impression is that supposed idea derived?* And if it be impossible to assign any,
this will serve to confirm our suspicion" (ibid., p. 22).
   Only suspicious characters, it appears, are threatened by this
challenge. For in the *Treatise* Hume does not shrink from arguing,

from the manifest legitimacy of one particular unsuspect idea, to the existence of its proper and necessary parent impression: "Now 'tis certain we have an idea of extension; for otherwise why do we talk and reason concerning it?" (I (ii) 2, p. 32). That is, perhaps, all very well. So the first thing which we have to notice here, and to challenge, is Hume's uncritical assumption that ideas, conceived as mental images, must play an essential part in the significant employment of words. It appears that for Hume ideas, so conceived, just are thoughts, in the everyday sense, and that no word can be employed meaningfully unless the user either has, or is disposed to have, appropriate imagery.

The most illuminating way of enforcing this point is by noticing that, in paying tribute to "one of the greatest and most valuable discoveries that has been made of late years in the republic of letters", Hume understates Berkeley's achievement. For Berkeley in fact did more than assert "that all general ideas are nothing but particular ones, annexed to a certain term, which gives them a more extensive signification, and makes them recall upon occasion other individuals, which are similar to them" (THN I (i) 7, p. 17). For he argued, further, that words can be both used and understood without benefit of either the actual or the dispositional occurrence of any mental imagery at all (Berkeley, 1732, VII 14; and compare Flew, 1974).

The second thing to notice is that, while the distinction between impressions and ideas seems to be defined in terms of "the degrees of force and liveliness, with which they strike upon the mind," the contention that "all our ideas . . . are copies of our impressions" is presented, appropriately to Hume's declared scientific purpose: not as a made to measure truth, following from the definitions prescribed for its terms; but as a matter rather of contingent fact, which could conceivably have been other than it is here alleged to be. In order to sustain this psychologistic version of empiricism, Hume appeals to two sorts of evidence: first, examination of his own experience; and, second, the experience of those born blind, deaf or otherwise experientially defective. "Those", therefore, "who would assert that this position is not universally true nor without exception have only one, and that an easy method of refuting it; by producing that idea which, in their opinion is not derived from this source" (EHU II, p. 19).

But this – not to put too fine a point on it – is outrageous. It is all very well to support such a psychological generalization by citing the kind of evidence which Hume does cite, and then to challenge all comers to produce a counter-example. But it simply will not do at all to turn the generalization thus supported into the supposedly sure foundation of a method of challenge; dismissing anything which might be proffered as a counter-example as being, on that ground alone, necessarily discredited. He is arguing that, if we can find no impression of which some putative idea is a representation, then it cannot really be legitimate: ". . . if no impression can be produced, he concludes that the term is altogether insignificant" (*Abstract*, p. 649).

Yet even that is only the half of it. For, in making his original case for this psychological generalization, Hume admits "one contradictory phenomenon, which may prove that it is not absolutely impossible for ideas to arise, independent of their correspondent impressions". This is the case of the intermediate shade. Suppose that in a long life someone had enjoyed impressions of all but one of the shades of blue presented on some standard, graded and numbered shade card. (Perhaps his copy was missing the colour patch on space Number 10!) Then, surely, he could form an idea of that missing shade, as a cross between Numbers 9 and 11? Hume agrees, but is not disturbed: ". . . this instance is so singular, that it is scarcely worth our observing, and does not merit that for it alone we should alter our general maxim" (EHU II, p. 21).

That too is scandalous. For, notoriously, any universal generalization is decisively falsified by even one single genuine counter-example. Such knock-down falsification is not to be disregarded as "so singular, that it is scarcely worth our observing". Hume's "general maxim" is thus trumped by Francis Bacon's ace: "Praestat vis instantiae negativae!"

Something sounder can, nevertheless, be developed from Hume's heads-I-win-tails-you-lose procedure. The psychological can be transmuted into a philosophical thesis – and this provides a paradigm of the sort of transposition which is often rewarding to the student of Hume. Consider Hume's own example of the man blind from birth. The psychological thesis is that, because he has never enjoyed visual sensations, he is unable to form visual mental images. This may well be true. But how was Hume in a position to know? He of all people cannot afford to allow, what is in any event not true, that matters of contingent psychological fact may be known apriori. For had he not himself insisted, in his Introduction to the *Treatise*, that: "As the science of man is the only solid foundation for the other sciences, so the only solid foundation we can give to this science itself must be laid on experience and observation" (p. xvi)?

Suppose now that someone who had been blind from birth did sometimes have coloured mental images. It is conceivable. But how, if he had never been able to see any yellow things, could he himself identify them as coloured or share his findings with us? At one moment the *Treatise* does get very warm. It is also the first of several occasions in Hume's writings where two expressions linked by the phrase "or, in other words," are not merely not the same in meaning but instead are relevantly and quite crucially different: "To give a child an idea of scarlet or orange, of sweet or bitter, I present the objects, or, in other words, convey to him these impressions" (I(i) 1, p. 5).

The crux is that a person blind from birth, even if they were to enjoy visual mental imagery, could not describe any of its purely visual characteristics in any language shared with the more fortunate rest of us. This is because the meanings of purely visual terms – such as 'green' or 'yellow' – and of the visual elements in the meanings of partly visual terms – such as 'iridescent' and 'shady' – can be explained and understood only by reference to visible features of the External World. If now we generalize this we get a principle which, by a natural yet noteworthy extension of the meaning of the qualifying adjective, we shall call etymological empiricism. No word can be understood by anyone unless its meaning can somehow be given in terms of their experience, and no term can have any public meaning in a public language except what can be given by reference to the public world. Such a principle is logical, not psychological. Its truth, if it is true, depends not on whether certain contingent facts obtain about people, but entirely on the meanings of the terms employed to state it.

To enforce the general point more firmly, reconsider the particular question of visual ideas enjoyed by those never vouchsafed visual impressions. Suppose that we wish to test Hume's general hypothesis by reference to this particular case. We enlist the cooperation of a team of persons blind from birth. They come trooping into our psychological laboratory, eager to serve as respondents to our questions, or subjects in our experiments. But then what next? Suppose further – what we all probably believe to be practically impossible – that some or all of them have in fact enjoyed such visual imagery. Then they will still not be able to tell us anything about its purely visual characteristics.

Even upon the yet wilder supposition that some or all of them guessed which of the colour words which they had heard sighted people employing were correctly applicable to which parts of their own mental imagery, still they could not know, and therefore neither could we know, that their guesses were correct. What and all that they could tell us, and what and all we could in consequence know, is that they were enjoying a kind of image experience as different from tactual, auditory, olfactory and gustatory as each of these is from every other. But from this alone we could not become entitled to infer that it was visual. For, for all that we or they could at that stage know, it might be imagery of an altogether fresh and unfamiliar kind; perhaps of a kind appropriate to, or 'belonging to', a genuine sixth and extra sense (Flew, 1953, p. 113; but compare Flew, 1986).

There is indeed only one way in which the situation could be saved. They would know, and we could know, that their strange mental imagery was visual, and that it was characterized in such purely visual ways; on one condition. That one necessary and sufficient condition is that – thanks perhaps to new surgical operations exploiting dramatic advances in technique – they became sighted, and were able at last to learn the visual vocabulary in the way in which the rest of us learnt it. They would, that is to say, learn how to apply such words as 'yellow' and 'red', both to ideas and to impressions, by first learning the conventions for their application to objects in the External World.

What earlier we distinguished as a principle of etymological empiricism could serve Hume's methodological purposes admirably. Indeed it presumably was because he was groping for something on these lines, and felt so certain that there is hereabouts something absolutely crucial and right, if only he could find the formulation, that he waved away what, against what he was actually saying, were decisive objections. Such a principle of etymological empiricism could, where a psychological generalization could not, support his challenges to explain in terms of human experience the meanings of allegedly significant expressions. It could also spare him some of the embarrassments to which his psychological empiricism gave rise.

Thus, in the *Treatise*, Hume distinguishes simple from complex perceptions. He insists that whereas complex ideas do not have to be copies of complex impressions the simple ideas of which they are composed can only be derived from simple impressions. The relevant analogue would be a distinction between terms which can be defined verbally and terms which can be defined only ostensively. Once this replacement is made the problem of the impressionless idea of the intermediate shade disappears. For, whereas the idea of that shade would have to be simple, the word for it would equally obviously, be definable, as indeed it is by Hume defined, in terms of the ostensively defined words for the two adjacent shades, Numbers 9 and 11.

It is, before moving on to the different topic of our knowledge or our lack of knowledge of the External World, worth noticing certain differences between the treatments in the *Treatise* and in the first *Enquiry*. The former makes much of ideas as essential to the significant and understanding employment of words, whereas the latter largely drops this. The *Treatise* speaks of ideas as "exact representations" of impressions (I (i) 1, p. 3). But although the first *Enquiry* still says "that all our ideas . . . are copies of our impressions" (II, p. 19), the point is not pressed in the literal, psychologizing way in which it was pressed in Part II of Book I of the *Treatise*. That part indeed, seems to have sunk almost without trace in the writing of the later book.

Again, while the *Treatise* takes it that impressions are always and only involved in actually feeling and seeing – and ideas in merely imagining, remembering or thinking – officially their only, and hence presumably defining difference lies in their different vivacity. The maximum concession in the *Treatise* to disturbing facts, such as eidetic and hallucinatory imagery or auditory percepts so faint as to be mistaken for imagings, is therefore: "that in particular instances" ideas and impressions "may very nearly approach to each other" (I (i) 1, p. 2). In the first *Enquiry*, however, although the "two classes . . . are distinguished by their different degrees of force", this distinction seems to be regarded not so much as defining as a contingent accompaniment of the fundamental division between thinking and experience. Thus the later book can afford to concede that in "disease or madness" ideas and impressions can become "altogether indistinguishable" (II, p. 17).

Again, this *Enquiry* contains hints of a fresh distinction, between language and the world: "All the colours of poetry . . . can never . . . make the description be taken for a real landskip" (II, p. 17). Nor should we overlook that the paragraphs which take the place of discussion of simple and complex ideas entertain the incongruously Cartesian thought: "What never was seen . . . may yet be conceived; nor is anything beyond the power of thought, except what implies an absolute contradiction" (II, p. 18). (This was a point which in *Meditation VI* Descartes had illustrated in a way which we might have hoped would prove unforgettable: he could both conceive and image a triangle; but a chiliagon he could only conceive.)

Of course, all this is largely a matter of nuances. Yet it does suggest that the mature Hume was beginning to edge away from his first extreme and rather unstable form of psychological empiricism. He seems to be recognizing some of its inadequacies and, perhaps, realizing that the really fruitful point is that the range of human understanding must be limited ultimately by the range of human experience: "though our thought seems to possess . . . unbounded liberty . . . it is really confined within very narrow limits . . . all this creative power of the mind amounts to no more than the faculty of compounding, transposing, augmenting, or diminishing the materials afforded us by the senses and experience" (EHU II, p. 19).

## 2 MIND-DEPENDENT AND MIND-INDEPENDENT REALITIES

So perhaps Hume was at least beginning to move from the assumption that meaning and understanding are matters of forming or being able to form mental imagery, and towards some notion that the keys lie in abilities and dispositions to speak and to behave. But certainly, and most unlike either Locke or Berkeley, Hume never became much interested in questions which he saw as concerned with words and their meanings: for him, as for too many others, to say verbal was to say merely verbal; and, hence, trifling (EHU VII (i), pp. 80-1). Equally certainly, and more to the present point, Hume never abandoned two fundamental convictions: first, that all we are or can be aware of is "the perceptions of the human mind"; and, second, that given these as our only data, it is impossible to make valid inferences about the characteristics or even the existence of any mind-independent realities, any External World. The first of these principles is the second of his three Cartesian fundamentals while the second is a particular application of the first of those fundamentals.

The importance of the second of these convictions is mainly in its application to one particular kind of "perceptions"; those impressions, namely, which Locke or Berkeley would have picked out as ideas of sense, or sensory or sensible ideas, and which in our century are usually labelled sensa, sense-data or percepts. All these various terms and expressions are, or ought to be, so defined that it becomes impossible: from premises referring solely to sense-data – or whatever else you choose to call them; validly to deduce any conclusions about any mind-independent realities – which may or may not have caused their subjects to have those sense-data. It is, therefore, unfortunate, even if perhaps unavoidable, that everyone insists upon employing in this connection terms which, in their ordinary usage, carry implications of precisely that sort which the chief sponsors of the concept of the sense-datum have specifically desired to disown.

The difficulty is that the ordinary and primary usage of such perceptual words as 'see' or hear' is to claim their own particular kind of cognitive success. If I assert that I am able to see this or to hear that, and if it is then revealed that there was and is no this to be seen or that to be heard, then such a revelation is sufficient to demonstrate that I did not in fact see this or hear that. So it was a case: not of my seeing, but of my (sneer) 'seeing' this; not of my hearing, but of my (sneer) 'hearing' that. It is for the same reason that it must be wrong to speak, as so many have in fact so wrongly spoken, either of perceiving sense-data or of perceiving any other "perceptions of the human mind". For these are precisely not mind-independent realities which a subject might seek to perceive or might try not to perceive, might succeed in perceiving or might manage not to perceive. They are, rather, events which happen to people, events of which apart from the people to whom they happen it makes no sense to talk.

Consider, for instance, such "perceptions of the human mind" as stabs of stomach pain or thrills of sexual pleasure. (It is, after all, bodily sensations rather than sense-data which leap first to mind when, on page 1 of the *Treatise*, Hume lists "sensations" along with "passions and emotions" as the first of three sorts of impressions.) If once the pains or the thrills are upon you there is, we might say, no room in logical space for attempts to avoid feeling those pains or to succeed in feeling those thrills; although there remains, of course, plenty of room for trying beforehand to get into positions where you will not have the one or will have the other. (Men, living under

Bentham's two masters of pain and pleasure, are doing it all the time.) Again, to put the same thing in another way, it makes no sense to report upon bodily sensations in the terms applicable to pieces of portable property. Books, for instance, can be mislaid, stolen, given away, stored, burnt, rebound, transported or subjected to any number of other physical operations; operations to which such mind-dependent realities as sense-data or painful sensations yield no purchase whatsoever.

Having explained what is meant by the term 'sense-datum' and its equivalents or near-equivalents, as well as by the expressions 'mind-dependent reality' and 'mind-independent reality', and before proceeding to consider where Hume was led by his two fundamental convictions about "perceptions of the human mind", it is necessary to dispose of the contrary contention that Hume did in fact contrive to rid himself of these commitments. For in a recent book on *Hume's Philosophy of Common Life* – a book most valuable for its demonstration that Hume rather than Burke ought to be recognized as the founder of the modern conservative intellectual tradition – the author, after conceding "that Hume inherited Locke's 'new way of ideas' . . .", goes on to maintain that a "radically different and distinctively Humean" usage of the term 'perception' is to be found "not presented at the outset of the *Treatise* but . . . virtually buried some 200 pages later in what are notoriously the most difficult sections . . ." (Livingston, 1984, p. 10).

If this is right then every previous interpreter must have been wrong, including the only person to have devoted an entire – and much respected – book to precisely those "notoriously . . . most difficult sections" (Price, 1940a). In particular Thomas Reid will be shown to have devoted most of his professional life to the dismembering of a straw man. For, as the same radical right-wing dissident had observed a few years earlier, "Reid took Hume's work to be a reduction to absurdity of a philosophical hypothesis which began in modern times with Descartes . . . 'The hypothesis I mean is, that nothing is perceived but what is in the mind which perceives it . . .'" (Livingston, 1976, p. 2).

Now certainly Hume does often write in a way hard or even impossible to reconcile with the views which Reid attributed to him, and that not only in those four sections in the final Part IV of Book I of the *Treatise* (I (iv) 2-4 and 7). We have already noticed, in the previous section of the present chapter, that, in the very first section of Part I of Book I, he brazenly identifies producing an impression with producing an object: "To give a child an idea of scarlet or orange, of sweet or bitter, I present the objects, or, in other words, convey to him these impressions." But then, in the concluding section 7 of that book, Hume himself suggests that anyone who spoke and acted in every way and always consistently with his own first philosophical findings would become an intolerably alienated pariah.

For a refutation of the suggestion that Hume eventually jettisoned these two principles, we have to turn to the first *Enquiry*. Of course, we cannot so far respect Hume's wishes as to ignore the *Treatise*; any more than Berkeley scholars can ignore the surviving draft for the Introduction to the *Principles*, or the notebooks now known as the *Philosophical Commentaries*. But that is no reason to rush to the opposite extreme, by ignoring the mature works by which Hume himself asked to be judged. Yet that is what, at least on the present count, Donald Livingston appears to have done. For he has ignored section XII of the first *Enquiry*; which is the one which reworks and adorns materials from Part IV of Book I of the *Treatise*.

There we find two decisive proof-texts. First, there is the statement that "the slightest philosophy . . . teaches us, that nothing can ever be present to the mind but an image or perception, and that the senses are only the inlets, through which these images are conveyed, without being able to produce any immediate intercourse between the mind and the object." Second, after offering, as "the obvious dictates of reason", the thesis "that the existences, which we consider, when we say, *this house* and *that tree*, are nothing but perceptions in the mind, and fleeting copies or representations of other existences, which remain uniform and independent", Hume insists that we cannot legitimately infer, from what we have since been taught to call sense-data, conclusions about such "other existences" – existences, that is, additional to, independent of and somehow behind those sense-data. For "to justify this pretended philosophical system, by a chain of clear and convincing argument, or even any appearance of argument, exceeds the power of all human capacity" (EHU XII (i), p. 152).

This is the reason why we have in what Henry Price called *Hume's Theory of the External World*: not a philosophical account of what and how we can know; but instead a seminal inquiry into the causes producing those beliefs which we do in fact have. Hume is thus giving us an exploratory essay in what present-day practitioners, notwithstanding that they are themselves all the while professing total professional neutrality with regard to the cognitive status of all beliefs thus sociologized, perversely insist upon describing as the sociology of knowledge (Berger and Luckmann, 1971, Introduction; and compare Flew, 1982). Hume's labours to show, both here and still more in the *Natural History of Religion*, "that ideas emerge systematically out of other ideas, for example out of tensions between conflicting ideas", are examples of something more "usually associated with such philosophers as Hegel and Marx" (Fogelin, 1985, p. 80).

About the "principle concerning the existence of body" knowledge, according to Hume, is unattainable: ". . . he cannot pretend by any arguments of philosophy to maintain its veracity." So, for the man of sense, there is no alternative save to inhibit inclinations to Pyrrhonian scepticism, and to welcome the irresistible Panzerwaffe of natural belief as it punches through the flimsy fancies of the Veil of Appearance: "Nature has not left this to his choice . . . We may well ask, *What causes induce us to believe in the existence of body*? but 'tis in vain to ask, *Whether there be body or not*? That is a point, which we must take for granted in all our reasonings" (THN I (iii) 2, p. 187).


## 3 THE "MONSTROUS OFFSPRING"

If we accept the truth of the two fundamental convictions distinguished at the beginning of the previous section, then certainly we must allow that no "arguments of philosophy" can sustain "the principle concerning the existence of body". Hume has several strong and sound things to say about attempts to establish that conclusion in ways consistent with those convictions: for instance, he sees off the entire Cartesian system in a single short paragraph (EHU XII (i), p. 153). But the main philosophical profit to be got from Hume's answer to the question 'What causes induce us to believe in the existence of body?' – an answer which, since it is to be found only in the *Treatise*, he would in his later years have wished us to ignore – lies in its unintended suggestions that and how those convictions themselves should have been challenged.

(i) In the first place Hume writes, here and always, as if we were all in it together, sharing the same cognitive predicament. Even in the famous final section of Book I he complains only of "that forelorn solitude, in which I am plac'd in my philosophy, and fancy myself some strange uncouth monster, who . . . has been expell'd all human commerce, and left utterly abandon'd and disconsolate". (I (iv) 7, p. 264). Yet, upon the principles supposedly made manifest "by the slightest philosophy", his situation must be immeasurably worse than that thus gloomily pictured. For, if he cannot know that there are any mind-independent objects in an External World – which upon those principles there is no denying but that he cannot – then most certainly there is no knowing that included among those are many other persons. The true and inescapable outcome is epistemological solipsism: no one can know that the Universe contains anything or anyone other than himself (or herself, or itself).

Suppose that Hume were to reply that persons, or people, are not at all that sort of thing. We are not, as we might uninstructedly have thought, creatures of flesh and blood. Instead we are, or he is, "nothing but a bundle or collection of different perceptions , which succeed each other with inconceivable rapidity, and are in a perpetual flux and movement" (THN I (iv) 6, p. 252). This, if possible, makes the situation even worse. For if, "properly speaking, 'tis not our body we perceive, when we regard our limbs and members, but certain impressions . . .", then how could we hope to perceive or otherwise to learn about, such, because incorporeal, in principle unperceivable entities as bundles or collections of perceptions?

A further difficulty, to which we shall return, is that to suggest that there are, or that we might be, bundles or collections of sense-data and other kinds of "perceptions of the human mind" makes no more sense than to suggest that someone might collect and bundle up the previously "loose and separate" surviving grins of several Cheshire cats long since disappeared (Carroll, 1865, ch. VI, p. 67; and compare Carroll, 1872, ch. IX, p. 223). The reason is that sense-data and other "perceptions of the human mind" are mind-dependent, or, rather, person-dependent; just as grins on the faces of Cheshire cats are Cheshire cat-dependent. To say that someone has or enjoys or suffers or experiences a sense-datum just is to say that that person is affected in a particular way; and such affections cannot significantly be separated from the persons thus affected. (That is why it is so totally wrong to talk of perceiving sense-data or any other "perceptions of the human mind": what is properly and truly perceived must be ontologically independent of its perceiver.)

(ii) In the second place, again here and always, when speaking in so many words of appeals to or arguments from experience, Hume employs the word in its everyday sense. For instance: having made the point, presumably against Berkeley, that it is not "the involuntariness of certain impressions" but "a peculiar *constancy*, which distinguishes them from the impressions, whose existence depends upon our perception", Hume goes on to claim that this, that and the other is "conformable to my experience". Thus "I never have observ'd, that this noise cou'd proceed from anything but the motion of a door; and therefore conclude, that the present phaenomenon is a contradiction to all past experience, unless the door, which I remember on t'other side the chamber, be still in being" (THN I (iv) 2, pp. 194 and 196).

Once we have reminded ourselves of the ordinary sense of 'experience', and of the ordinary senses of the other key words in this passage, it becomes clear that Hume has no business to be arguing in this way. For in that ordinary and most useful sense a claim to have had experience of something is a claim to have been in direct contact with mind-independent realities; whereas Hume is supposed to be committed to the contentions that he, and we, are never so privileged as to be granted any such close and cognitive contacts with an or the External World. He, therefore, is entitled to employ the word 'experience', and all other terms with similar meanings, with reference only to ongoings in his own mind – to his own Internal World, so to speak.

To bring out the enormous and vital difference between these two senses, consider the sad case of the philosophically scrupulous applicant, who responds to the advertisement of a farmer seeking to hire hands with experience of cows. In interview he, or she, has to admit that – despite having had both many dreams of cows and abundant cowish sense-data – he, or she, neither is nor ever will be in a position to know that there even are such things as cows. Such an applicant would be lucky simply to be dismissed from interview, without suffering any penalty for impertinence.

Enormous though the difference between the everyday (public) and the factitious (private) sense is, however, philosophers have all too often, even in contexts where it is vital, failed to make this distinction. For instance, from beginning to end of a long and devoutly painstaking book entitled *Our Experience of God*, the author never once recognizes that it is only from reports of religious experience, in the public sense of 'experience', that we might be able to draw valid conclusions about the existence and nature of God (H. D. Lewis, 1959; and compare Flew, 1966, ch. 6).

This given, we have also to distinguish corresponding senses of 'empiricism'. Taking 'based upon or derived from' to be the core idea, we can construe the thesis of logical empiricism as the claim that all knowledge – or, rather, all knowledge of contingent facts – must be somehow referred to experience. Our own new coinage 'etymological empiricism' is a label for the contention that all our concepts must be such as could be explained by reference to our experience.

Once again it is – once it has been forcefully pointed out – obvious that there are enormous differences between different doctrines of empiricism, depending upon which way they interpret the term 'experience'. If it is to be in the ordinary sense, then logical empiricism becomes, surely, a truism; albeit a truism of the last importance? But if it is to be in the mind-dependent, private sense, then verbally the same doctrine becomes, though perennially fascinating, ultimately preposterous. Yet once again we find a curious and curiously widespread failure to make and to insist upon the fundamental distinction. Even Fraser Cowley, in that lamentably neglected book *A Critique of British Empiricism*, does not make it in a direct and explicit way.

(iii) A third unintended suggestion arises when we bring into account a revealing remark already discussed in section 1 of the present chapter: "To give a child an idea of scarlet or orange, of sweet or bitter, I present the objects, or, in other words, convey to him these impressions . . ." (THN I (i) 1, p. 5). Transposed into the idiom of etymological empiricism, this tells us that in order to describe our mental imagery – or even, for that matter, our sense-data – we have to employ words the meanings of which can be explained and understood only by referring to features of the public, External World. It is literally preposterous to hold that we either should or can start from sure and unshakeable knowledge of our own (private) experience, and then try to move on from there to some knowledge of the Universe around us. For, on the contrary, the very formulation of any propositions about that (private) experience presupposes knowledge of supposedly forever inaccessible external reality.

In the *Treatise* discussion 'Of scepticism with regard to the senses' Hume redeploys two stock philosophical illustrations, concluding that from these, and from "an infinite number of other experiments of the same kind . . . we learn, that our sensible perceptions are not possest of any distinct or independent existence" (I (iv) 2, p. 211). In a less artificial terminology this amounts to saying that these Arguments from Illusion prove that there is in fact no such thing as perception; that we are never, that is to say, immediately aware through our senses of the existence and some of the characteristics of any mind-independent reality.

By thus showing that and how we are sometimes misled into sensory error, and by inferring from this that we can never truly and correctly perceive, Hume is presenting an argument of the same egregiously unsound form as that so memorably and so disturbingly unleashed by Descartes in the *Discourse*: ". . . because our senses sometimes deceive us, I wished to suppose that nothing is just as they cause us to imagine it to be; and because there are men who deceive themselves in their reasoning . . . I rejected as false all reasonings formerly accepted by me as demonstrations."

The form of these arguments is egregiously unsound in as much as the desired conclusions, not merely do not follow from, but are also actually incompatible with, the proferred premises. For if, in some area, we know some cases in which we have been mistaken; then we must have some knowledge, in that area, and cannot have been in every instance wrong. (One popular and parallel fallacy, in a quite different field, is that of arguing that, since everything must have a cause, and since the chain of causes allegedly cannot extend indefinitely backwards in time, therefore there must have been, in the beginning, a First Cause!) All this is bad enough; indeed very bad indeed. Nevertheless, as it now appears, that is by no means the whole of it.

For suppose that the sceptic about the External World learns from the mistakes of Descartes and Hume, and resolves that, in trying to make out his claim that we have no knowledge, there is to be no appeal to any knowledge of discovered perceptual errors. Then still, if this, third unintended suggestion is correct, the sceptic wanting to formulate and to utter his scepticism must presuppose some of that very knowledge which is to be denied. For what – to come to very particular cases – should we say of people who, confronted with a herd of cows or a collection of luminously valid and baby-simple arguments, protested that they had never for certain seen any cows or never for certain recognized any arguments to be valid? What else but that, always supposing their protests to be ingenuous, these nescients simply did not know the meanings of the word 'cow' or of the expression 'valid argument'?

(iv) The fourth unintended suggestion arises from considering a "philosophical system" described in the *Treatise* as "the monstrous offspring of two principles, which are contrary to each other, which are both at once embrac'd by the mind, and which are unable mutually to destroy each other". The principles are imagination and reflection, and – at the end of a gripping story involving a deal of self-deception, wishful-thinking and creative play – we are told: "The contradiction betwixt these opinions we elude by a new fiction, which is conformable to the hypotheses both of reflection and fancy, by ascribing these contrary qualities to different existences; the *interruption* to perceptions, and the *continuance* to objects" (I (iv) 2, p. 215).

Hume thus develops a psychogenetic account of what philosophers have since christened the Representative Theory of Perception. But this system, as he argues most forcefully in the first *Enquiry*, is rationally indefensible: "By what argument can it be proved, that the perceptions of the mind must be caused by external objects, entirely different from them, though resembling them (if that be possible), and could not arise either from the energy of the mind itself, or from the suggestion of some invisible and unknown spirit, or from some other cause still more unknown to us?" (XII (i), pp. 152-3: this mention of "some invisible and unknown spirit" is, presumably, another of Hume's rather rare references to the works of Berkeley).

What we need to notice about the contention offered next is that it takes for granted the "two fundamental convictions" distinguished at the beginning of the previous section of the present chapter: "The mind has never anything present to it but the perceptions, and cannot possibly reach any experience of their connexion with objects" (ibid., p. 153). Certainly, if all this be granted, then there can be no argument of experience to prove that any "perceptions of the mind" are ever "caused by external objects, entirely different from them".

For what is thus granted is pretty well equivalent to the conclusion desired.

Perhaps the reason why so many philosophers have been ready to agree that this conclusion is inescapable is that they have been thinking of attempts to establish it "By experience surely", but by the experience solely of single persons, probably incorporeal, and certainly working in solipsistic isolation (ibid., p. 153). Of course, if someone actually was thus totally alone in a solipsistic universe, then that someone might very well be unable to find any experiential reason for believing that external objects ever cause sense-data to be had, or that there is any sense in talking about resemblances between sense-data and objects. Perhaps the best, or the worst, that could be done by someone in those circumstances would be to reach a Representative Theory of Perception through following the intellectually disreputable course which, according to Hume, we have in fact followed in giving birth to that "monstrous offspring".

But in the actual human situation, the naturally social character of which Hume himself is normally most eager to emphasize, it becomes perfectly possible for one person to observe and to experiment on another person's perceivings. The one who thus really is introducing "the experimental method of reasoning into moral subjects" can both perceive the objects perceived by the other and receive that other's reports upon the sense-data involved in that perceiving. By suitable manipulations of those objects the experimenter can demonstrate the causal relations subsisting between them and the sense-data reported. Furthermore, and to no one's surprise, descriptions of the sense-data will frequently be found to correspond very closely with descriptions of the objects causing those sense-data to occur. All this, surely, adds up to as good an argument as could be desired: showing that at least some "perceptions of the mind" in fact are "caused by external objects, entirely different from them, though resembling them"; and also showing how such representative resemblance "be possible".

(v) The fifth and final unintended suggestion concerns the confounding of scientific with philosophical questions. Hume spends little space upon "the more trite topics, employed by the sceptics in all ages, against the evidence of *sense*" (EHU VII (i), p. 151). So there is no call for us to review an array of what are nowadays labelled Arguments from Illusion (Austin, 1962a). However, as was emphasized in chapter 1, Hume saw all his works as contributions to "moral subjects", which certainly included what since Hartley has been known as psychology (Passmore, 1952, p. 4). So it is to the point to notice how Hume fails to distinguish: questions about the mechanisms involved in perception; from questions about what it must mean to say that something has been perceived.

Thus he never manages outright to state that perception necessarily involves, or would involve, immediate awareness of the mind-independent realities allegedly perceived. Hence he never draws the shocking consequence that, on his view and that of many like-minded philosophers of perception, there simply is no such thing. Instead, in representing "the conclusions, which the vulgar form on this head", he prefers to maintain: not that they think – mistakenly in his philosopher's view – that they often suceed in perceiving; but that they "confound perceptions and objects, and attribute a distinct continu'd existence to the very things they feel and see" (THN I (iv) 2, p. 193).

Soon, in a crescendo of collapsing distinctions, supposedly in order both to "avoid all ambiguity and confusion on this head" and "to accommodate myself to their notions", Hume announces that he is going temporarily to concede "that there is only a single existence, which I shall call indifferently *object* or *perception* . . . understanding by both of them what any common man means by a hat, or a shoe, or stone, or any other impression convey'd to him by his senses" (ibid., p. 202).

But "the vulgar", of course, have never heard tell of sense-data at all; and, were we to introduce them to those exotic entities, they would in the most categorical fashion repudiate any suggestion that that was the sort of thing which they mean "by a hat, or a shoe, or stone".

Again, it is the considering of outline accounts of the mechanisms of perception which helps to mislead Hume, as it has helped to mislead so many others both before and since, into giving false analyses of perceptual concepts. For, surely, the physiological investigations of Descartes were part of that "slightest philosophy, which teaches us, that nothing can ever be present to the mind but an image or perception, and that the senses are only the inlets, through which these images are conveyed, without being able to produce any immediate intercourse between the mind and the object" (EHU XII (i), p. 152)?

To the question whether perception occurs, and whether it involves "immediate intercourse between the mind and the object", we have to respond, like the man asked whether he believed in baptism by total immersion: 'But of course I believe in it. I've seen it done.' And how could anyone be more immediately aware of anything than by having it available bang in front of them under ideal conditions, and being fully able to see it, touch it, and what have you?

The trouble is that, by contemplating the sense-organs and the nerves linking these with the brain, people are tempted to think that all that is ever perceived is sense-data, presented perhaps in the pineal gland. But the truth is that the only things which can properly be said to be perceived are physical objects, and other features of mind-independent reality. Although in perceiving we may, indeed must, have sense-data, these cannot themselves significantly be said to be objects of perception. Since "perceptions of the mind" cannot be perceived at all, it is certain that we cannot perceive only and nothing but such 'perceptions'.

# 3

# Infinite Divisibility, Mathematics and Hume's Fork

Part II of Book I of the *Treatise* is by common consent the least satisfactory – perhaps it is also the least satisfactory in all Hume's publications. He himself when he came to compose the first *Enquiry* found little here fit for salvage: what he did reuse is almost all crammed into Part II of Section XII. But although the later essay shows that he no longer wanted to make much of these discussions, it also indicates that he did not completely abandon some of the most questionable contentions put forward in "that juvenile work". In particular he was not able to bring himself wholly to reject two favourite notions: that conceiving must require the forming of some sort of mental image; and that it is absurd to assert that anything finite might be infinitely divisible.

Both of these notions are essentially involved in the account, in the later work, of how "The chief objection against all *abstract* reasonings is derived from the ideas of space and time . . ." Hume wants to turn this sceptical onslaught round, so that it can no longer be used as a weapon by propounders of "priestly *dogmas*, invented on purpose to tame and subdue the rebellious reason of mankind . . ." So he concludes "that nothing can be more sceptical, or more full of doubt and hesitation, than this scepticism itself, which arises from some of the paradoxical conclusions of geometry or the science of quality" (XII (ii), pp. 156, 156 and 158).

In this account the notion that it is absurd to assert that anything finite might be infinitely divisible appears only in the form of an insistence upon the true absurdity of what Hume mistakes to be a consequence: that everything finite in fact consists in an infinite number of parts; each of which in turn consists in an infinite number of infinitely smaller parts; and so ad infinitum. The notion that conceiving must always require the forming of some sort of mental images comes out most clearly in a long note in which Hume hints at a way in which the paradoxes might perhaps be removed or resolved, and mathematics thus spared "the ridicule and contempt of the ignorant". He hopes to save the day by again summoning up one of Berkeley's suggestions but, as before, the one which still preserves the assumption that to have an idea must always involve forming an appropriate mental image: ". . . all general ideas are, in reality, particular ones, attached to a general term, which recalls, upon occasion, other particular ones, that resemble, in certain circumstances, the idea, present to the mind" (ibid., p. 158n). We shall, presumably, never know whether it was this suggestion which Hume developed in the essay "on the metaphisical principles of geometry" which he had intended to publish as one of the *Four Dissertations* in 1757, but which he suppressed, on the advice of his good mathematician friend Lord Stanhope (Greig, 1932, II, p. 253).

## 1 THE IMPOSSIBILITY OF FINITE INFINITES

The title of Part II is 'Of the ideas of space and time'. From that title, and from the fact that this part follows a discussion 'Of ideas; their origin, composition, abstraction, connexion, etc.', we should expect Hume's first concern here to be the development of an account of these two important ideas, according with the fundamental principle *"That all our simple ideas in their first appearance are deriv'd from simple impressions, which are correspondent to them, and which they exactly represent"* (I (i) 3, p. 4). Remembering the promises of the Introduction, we might maybe expect to hear after that of some alleged consequences for Mathematics, Natural Philosophy or Natural Religion.

Certainly before the part is over all these expectations are in some fashion fulfilled. Thus in section 3 Hume enquires after "the model, from which the idea of space is deriv'd" (p. 33); and, having found a solution which satisfies him, he proceeds to present an analogous answer to the parallel question about the idea of time. (About these sketchy attempts at solutions perhaps all which needs to be said here is that, if they did ever become available to Kant, they may have encouraged his own conviction that these two notions are not, after all, derivable from experience.)

Next under the heading 'Objections answered' in section 4, Hume outlines a consequential story about the nature and limitations of geometrical thinking; before, as 'The same subject continued', trying to meet three objections to the implication "that we can form no idea of a vacuum, or space, where there is nothing visible or tangible" (p. 53). What ought to be surprising is: that, instead of plunging straightway into the search for the impression or impressions from which each of these fundamental and rather special ideas may be derived, Hume starts by examining "the doctrine of infinite divisibility"; and that the account which he later gives of these ideas is presented as a consequence of his conclusions about infinite divisibility: "The other part of our system is a consequence of this" (pp. 26 and 39).

To understand why this Part II starts from, and gives so much attention to, questions about infinite divisibility we have to recognize two things. First, what were taken to be the absurdities and contradictions of and arising from this notion had – thanks especially to such propounders of "priestly *dogmas*" as the authors of the Port-Royal *Logic* – become cherished instruments for taming the presumption of secular reason; and Hume was no friend of any doctrinally substantial religion. (For the historical background see Kemp Smith, 1941, ch XIV; also Flew, 1968.) Second, if this notion is indeed contradictory and absurd then that must put geometry in jeopardy; and Hume had in his Introduction promised to do all he could to remedy "the present imperfection of the sciences" (p. xvii). We need to recognize that Hume saw his *Treatise* accounts both of the ideas of space and time and of the nature of geometrical thinking as – whatever their other merits or demerits – corollaries of what seemed to him to be the only possible escape from these disastrous contradictions and absurdities. This is necessary, if we are fully and sympathetically to appreciate how Hume was able there to present such incredibilities so confidently; and, further, why, although he later sketches a far better account of both pure and applied geometry, there are, nevertheless, backslidings.

Hume opens his argument by laying down two principles. Both he mistakes to be obvious: although one is true, surely, only in his own highly artificial interpretation; while the other is without qualification false. Certainly both are for him fundamental. The first is "that the capacity of the mind is limited, and can never attain a full and adequate conception of infinity . . ." This is the same as the ninth axiom given in chapter VII of Part IV of the Port-Royal *Logic*: "Il est de la nature d'un esprit fini de ne pouvoir comprendre l'infini" (Arnauld, 1662, p. 324). But that, so far from being as Hume has it "universally allowed", was as "Mens nostra, eo quod finita sit, nihil certi scire potest de infinito", on the list of Cartesian propositions condemned by the Jesuits. In Hume's formulation, straightforwardly interpreted, it is surely untrue. For there is no insuperable difficulty about learning the ordinary uses of the words 'infinite' and 'infinity', and we can perfectly well understand what is meant by talk of a series being infinite or going on to infinity. But, of course, Hume is not construing the expression "attain a full and adequate conception" in any such studiously simple-minded and pedestrian way. For – forgetting or rejecting the lessons taught by Descartes with the conceived chiliagon – Hume equates conceiving with imagining, and mistakes it that to imagine – or at any rate to be able to imagine – is always to form – or at any rate to be able to form – the appropriate mental image or images. Of course, if an idea of infinity has to be a mental image of the actual infinite, then indeed his conclusion does become just obvious.

The second of Hume's fundamentals, though it is presented as equally obvious, is in fact false: "whatever is capable of being divided *in infinitum*, must consist in an infinite number of parts . . ." (p. 26). This, though it struck him, and has struck many others even among the great, as a self-evident truth, is mistaken twice over. First, less importantly, to say that something is divisible into so many parts is not to say that it consists in – that it is, so to speak, already divided into – that number of parts. A cake may be divisible into many different numbers of equal slices without its thereby consisting in, through already having been divided into, any particular number of such slices. Second, absolutely crucially, to say that something may be divided in infinitum is not say that it can be divided into an infinite number of parts. It is rather, to say that it can be divided, and subdivided, and sub-sub-divided as anyone wishes: infinitely, without limit. That this is so is part of what is meant by the saying 'Infinity is not a number'!

The scandalous contradictions and absurdities are all generated by the same widely seductive falsism; and, once that is rejected, they all disappear. For, were it true, and were any finite thing then said to be infinitely divisible, then this would indeed imply that that finite thing was constituted of infinite collections of other finite things, which in turn are constituted of infinite collections of infinitely smaller finite things, and so on ad infinitum.

There is no need for us to follow Hume down the byways and blind alleys into which he was misled through making the two assumptions from which Part II began. (But compare, again, Flew, 1968). Yet it should be noticed, as it rarely has been, that this part contains conclusions which Hume presumably thought would demonstrate how "Even . . . Natural Philosophy" is "in some measure dependent on the science of MAN" (p. xix). So it seems that even the hard sciences – even the paradigm hard science, physics – are not altogether immune from that "present imperfect condition". For, under the disarming title 'Objections answered', section 4 begins with a suggestion that Hume's conclusions, which he has so far confined largely to the realm of ideas and impressions, must have drastic applications to the physical world. Since "whatever the mind clearly conceives includes the idea of possible existence" it must be "possible for space and time to exist conformable to this idea. And, if it be possible, 'tis certain they actually do exist conformable to it; since their infinite divisibility is utterly impossible and contradictory" (p. 39).

Hume is, surely, absolutely right in thus claiming that a thesis of the inconceivability of the infinite divisibility of any finite thing must have ontological implications, and at fault only, if at all, in not spelling out more boldly just what and how wide these implications would be? For such a thesis amounts to the contention that continuous magnitudes are – shall we say? – metaphysically impossible; and hence that every divisible finite existent, whether mind-depentent or mind-independent, must consist of a finite number of elements. (This is certainly a most drastic form of that atomism of which a much earlier generation of critics were forever accusing Hume; although what they usually had in the front of their minds was the implicit suggestion that ideas and impressions could be exactly counted.) Furthermore, Hume presumably is also committed by the same thesis to insisting in general that the ultimate elements constituting any particular sort of magnitude cannot themselves possess whatever is the characteristic in question: the indivisible points supposedly composing space cannot themselves have extension; the atomic moments of time must themselves be without duration; and so on.

These are very high, wide, and handsome metaphysical findings. They must put any philosophical reader in mind of such classical

Rationalists as Leibniz (Cottingham, 1984); and they scarcely consist with any stock pictures of Hume – including his own. They must, if correct, require extremely extensive "changes and improvements" even in "Natural Philosophy" (p. xix). We need not be surprised if it seems that Hume, the admirer and would-be imitator of Newton, is a little reluctant to expatiate upon – or even to notice – the full extent of such ontological implications. Certainly he contrives not to draw, but rather to disclaim, what for him would appear to be the clear consequences of saying "that we can form no idea of a vacuum . . ." (I (ii) 5, p. 53).

## 2 GEOMETRY AND THE GREAT DIVIDE

With respect to the implications for geometry, however, Hume at this stage suffered no similar inhibitions. His findings then were that, although the propositions of that discipline excel "the imperfect judgements of our senses and imagination", they fall "short of that perfect precision and certainty, which are peculiar to arithmetic and algebra . . ." (I (iii) 1, p. 71). This Humian story about geometry may be compared with the hard-pressed account of the nature of all mathematics given by J. S. Mill in *A System of Logic*. It is perhaps also worth noticing that it seems to have been taken up by Maupertuis, and to have had some part in shaping the mathematical opinions of the French Encyclopaedists (Laird, 1932, pp. 77-8).

The trouble with geometry, in Hume's *Treatise* view, is that "its original and fundamental principles are deriv'd merely from appearances . . ." (I (iii) 1, p. 71). This follows from his fundamental contentions about ideas and impressions. For if the ideas of 'circle', 'straight line', 'point', and so on are to be construed as mental images, then they simply cannot be the ideal notions of pure mathematics. Even a mental picture of a point must have extension as well as position. This comes out excellently in his challenge to "our mathematician to form, as accurately as possible, the ideas of a circle and a right line . . . I then ask if upon the conception of their contact he can conceive them as touching in a mathematical point, or if he must necessarily imagine them to concur for some space" (I (ii) 4, p. 53). Unable to see how ideal geometrical concepts could be derived from experience or how any concepts could occur without mental imagery, Hume had no option but to argue that really there is no such creature as an ideal geometrical notion.

He rams this moral home in an aggressive concluding paragraph: " 'Tis usual with mathematicians, to pretend, that those ideas, which are their objects, are of so refin'd and spiritual a nature, that they fall not under the conception of the fancy, but must be comprehended by a pure and intellectual view, of which the superior faculties of the soul are alone capable . . . But to destroy this artifice, we need but reflect on that principle so often insisted on, *that all our ideas are copy'd from our impressions*" (ibid., p. 72).

That emphasis – as always unless contraindicated – is in the original; a fact to be noted by those trying to make out that Hume was not, at this stage, both identifying conception with imagination, and taking imagining necessarily to involve forming mental images. It is also interesting to compare Hume's first stand on this issue with that of Plato in *Phaedo*. Neither could see how such ideal notions could be derived from experience. But Plato, accepting and indeed insisting that we do possess them, argued that we must have had them already in a previous life. Others, agreeing about the impossibility of experiential derivation, but not about the possibility of personal pre-existence, have spoken of innate ideas or apriori concepts.

So much, then, for the *Treatise* story. Hume's second thoughts are tossed off as an illustrative aside in the course of expounding a distinction between two categories of "objects of human reason or enquiry . . ., to wit *Relations of Ideas*, and *Matters of Fact*". It is with this initial trumpet blast in section IV that the later versions begin to become clearly and considerably superior to their predecessors. Here geometry is put on exactly the same footing as arithmetic and algebra, whereas the *Treatise* saw "algebra and arithmetic as the only sciences, in which we can . . . preserve a perfect exactness and certainty" (I (iii) 1, p. 71).

So now examples "Of the first kind" – Relations of Ideas – are to be found in "the sciences of Geometry, Algebra and Arithmetic, and, in short, every affirmation which is either intuitively or demonstratively certain . . . Propositions of this kind are discoverable by the mere operation of thought, without dependence on what is anywhere existent in the universe . . ."

Matters of fact, on the other hand, "are not ascertained in the same manner, nor is our evidence of their truth, however great, of a like nature. The contrary of every matter of fact is still possible, because it can never imply a contradiction . . ." (EHU IV (i), p. 25). This distinction between "*Relations of Ideas*, and *Matters of Fact*" is now, in its aggressive employments, known as Hume's Fork.

In the *Treatise*, although a distinction on these lines is adumbrated in Book I (e.g. at (iii) 7, p. 95 and (iii) 11, p. 124), and developed a little in Book II ((iii) 10, pp. 448-9; and compare (iii) 3, p. 414), it is only set visibly to work in Book III. It serves there as a framework for the analysis of moral judgements ((i) 1, pp. 463ff.). The direction of movement is interesting. Perhaps it weighs against Kemp Smith's contention that "Books II and III of the *Treatise* are in date of first composition prior to the working out of the doctrines dealt with in Book I" (Kemp Smith 1941, p. vi). However, he could have continued to hold his position by maintaining that the development traced amounts to no more than a progressive precisification; suggesting that it might have been through the valuable exercise of summarizing the novelties of the first two books for the *Abstract* that Hume came to realize how crucial for those arguments the present distinction is. This is, of course, on both sides, all speculation. What is solidly there for all to see is the improvement in successive publications.

Hume's originality here lies not in the making of some distinction on these lines but rather: first, on its aggressive employments as a tool of analysis; and, second, the making of it by spelling out the ways in which propositions of the two different sorts may be known to be true or, as the case may be, false. Such a distinction is a commonplace in, for instance, Leibniz; who may well have been Hume's immediate source. But it is the epistemological emphasis and the distinctively aggressive employment which has earned the respectful nickname 'Hume's Fork'.

Once we have appreciated that this has to be judged as an instrument for intellectual dissection rather than as a pair of label types for attaching to already unequivocally identified members of one or other of two natural kinds, it becomes obvious that some frequently made objections – objections parallel to those even more frequently made against that analogous analytic tool, Hume's Law – are entirely beside the point. (Hume's Law forbids, as necessarily invalid, all attempts to deduce normative conclusions from premises purely neutral and factual.)

Certainly, it is not the case that all actual utterances fall immediately and effortlessly into one or other of the two categories thus distinguished. If they already did, then there would be little profit in urging that the distinction always can and always ought to be made. We must too challenge those who pretend that either of these two categorical distinctions cannot in the end be drawn, to explain how they would themselves – if indeed they would – demonstrate the invalidity of the innumerable unsound arguments which, by doing what now supposedly cannot be done, unfashionable old-timers exposed successfully (Quine, 1963).

The differentiae between "*Relations of Ideas*" and "*Matters of Fact*" are: that whereas the former can be known apriori, and cannot be denied without self-contradiction; the latter can be denied without self-contradiction, and can be known only aposteriori. (Here and always, except in verbatim quotations from other people, 'apriori' and 'aposteriori' are rendered thus as single unitalicized words: since these Latinisms were first landed as immigrants over a quarter of a millenium ago – in Berkeley's *Principles*! – it is over-time for their full naturalization.)

The Hume's Fork dichotomy, whatever Hume's own personal and hesitant backslidings, thus belongs unambiguously not to introspective psychology but to Logic or – if a wider description is preferred – to Logic and Scientific Method. It obtains between propositions, and has nothing to do with any kind of mental imagery. If propositions stating, or purporting to state, the relations of ideas were indeed about mental imagery, then the whole classification would collapse, with these too becoming propositions stating, or purporting to state, matters of fact. This needs to be said with emphasis. For some philosophers, even among the greatest, have needed to be reminded that matters even of universal introspective psychological fact are just as contingent and aposteriori as any other members of this Humian category.

Any remaining suspicion that the phrase "either intuitively or demonstratively certain" might be intended to allow room for some criterion of the truth of propositions about the relations of ideas other than the test of non-contradiction is at least eased when, later in the same book, Hume makes it clear that the distinction he has in mind is that between those necessary propositions whose truth can be known immediately from an understanding of the meanings of their terms, and those which "cannot be known . . . without a train of reasoning and enquiry." His example of the former is "*that where there is no property, there can be no injustice*", and of the latter "*That the square of the hypoteneuse is equal to the squares of the other two sides*" (EHU XII (iii), p. 163).

None of this provides, surely, any sufficient reason for suggesting that geometry consists in a system of synthetic apriori truths; truths, that is, which could not be known simply "according to the principle of analysis alone, namely the principle of contradiction" (Kant, 1783, p. 17)? Certainly "Kant's theory of mathematical synthesis, particularly in its most unhappy pictorializing aspect, had rather more in common with Hume's own first account of mathematics than with any of the rival views espoused by other classical philosophers" (Flew, 1961, p. 65). But in giving this second account Hume says nothing requiring us to construe trains of reasoning and enquiry as anything but devices for "recognizing tautology when it is complicated".

Perhaps we have here another of those affinities which Wittgenstein would not have thanked us for pointing out (Jones, 1982, pp. 3 and 176-88). For where, save in literary style, is the difference between: "Though there never were a circle or a triangle in nature, the truths demonstrated by Euclid would for ever retain their certainty and evidence" (EHU IV (i), p. 25); and "Our fundamental principle is that every question which can be decided at all by logic can be decided without more ado. (And if we get into a situation where we need to answer such a problem by looking at the world, this shows that we are on a fundamentally wrong track)" (Wittgenstein, 1921, p. 145)?

Before we finish with Hume's treatments of mathematics, we have to show how wrong it is to say: "His recorded statements strongly suggest that he did not understand that it is logically possible . . . to apply the theorems of pure geometry to the explanation of physical phenomena after the names of suitable empirical entities had been substituted for undefined terms" (Noxon, 1973, p. 116). For there is in the first *Enquiry* one often overlooked paragraph in which Hume gives an account of what, perhaps borrowing the expression from Francis Bacon, he calls "mixed mathematics". Every part of this, Hume .writes, proceeds on the supposition that certain laws are established by nature in her operations; and abstract reasonings are employed, either to assist experience in the discovery of these laws, or to determine their influence in particular instances . . . Thus, it is a law of motion, discovered by experience, that the moment or force of any body is in the compound ratio or proportion of its solid contents and its velocity . . . Geometry assists us in the application of this law . . ." (IV (i), p. 31).

This is all very thin. It is gauche too in its references to physics. Apparently also it leans both on Malebranche and on the 1728 edition of Ephraim Chambers' *Cyclopaedia, or Universal Dictionary of the Arts and Sciences* (Wright, 1983, pp. 117-8). But it is more a by-blow, offered rather as an incidental illustration, than a full-dress exposition. It does, however, have the heart of the matter in it; the insight most incisively expressed in Einstein's famous epigram, "As far as the laws of mathematics refer to reality, they are not certain, and as far as they are certain they do not refer to reality." (Einstein's word was 'certain', where Hume had had 'demonstratively certain', and others might prefer 'necessarily true'.)

## 3 PUTTING THE INSTRUMENT TO USE

The first employment provided is – thriftily – in the very expounding and vindicating of the fundamental distinction itself. Hume intends his two categories to be both mutually exclusive and together exhaustive. But he starts with two differentiae. One distinguishes according to whether the contradictory is or is not self-contradictory; the other according to whether its truth-value could or could not be known only by reference to experience. We therefore both need and are given argument to show that the application of these two different criteria must always yield the same results. In the course of this engagement Hume expounds his mature view of the nature of and the difference between pure and applied mathematics; and it is its successful outcome, he believes, which enables him finally to assume the desired conclusions as incontestably truistic. So, in the *Dialogues*, we find both Cleanthes and Philo agreed: "that there is an evident absurdity in trying to demonstrate a matter of fact, or to prove it by any arguments *a priori*"; and that "Every event, before experience, is equally difficult; and every event, after experience, is equally easy and intelligible" (IX, p. 189; and VII, p. 182).

Curiously it appears that Hume never found occasion to employ his distinction between "*Matters of Fact*" and "*Relations of Ideas*" for exposing the fallaciousness of surreptitious shifts between two alternative interpretations of the same form of words. Such shifts from the one category to the other are in our time, especially in discussions of "moral subjects", extremely common, although perhaps in his day they were less so (Flew, 1975, ch. 3). Yet by using this distinction Hume might, for instance, have improved upon Butler's refutation of the denial of the possibility of disinterested action. (See, for instance, *Sermon XI*, ad init.) For that denial was, and frequently still is, sustained by an argument moving between two interpretations of such sentences as 'No one ever does anything which they do not want to do'. In one this is interpreted as, and is, a necessary truth. In the other it is interpreted as a contingent truth, but is in fact false. The nerve of the fallacy consists in arguing: from the necessary truth of the premise that every action proceeds from some motive, desire, or want – Relation of Ideas: to the conclusion, factually false, that none of us ever does anything we do not, in a more everyday less made-to-measure sense, want to do – Matter of Fact; or, strictly, not fact.

Certainly no one nowadays is fit to enter the field of the social sciences unless they are first both equipped and eager to press this distinction. Consider, for instance, one typical assertion in the *Communist Manifesto*: "The ruling ideas of each age have ever been the ideas of the ruling class" (Marx and Engels, 1848, p. 102; compare Flew, 1985, ch 5). If this is put forward as a contribution to social science, then we must demand to be told what criteria are proposed for identifying the ruling ideas of an age, and for doing so without either implicitly or explicitly assuming that these just are by definition the ideas cherished by whoever it is proposed to pick out as the members of the ruling class. Until and unless this challenge is met we shall have here only, and at best, tautology pretentiously misrepresented as sociological discovery.

What Hume himself saw as the possible profit promised by investigations into "the nature of that evidence which assures us of any real existence and matter of fact, beyond the present testimony of our senses, or the records of our memory" is something more important and heuristically more fruitful than an elegant technique for revealing the fallaciousness of one deplorably prevalent argument type. For such investigations, he continues modestly, "may even prove useful, by exciting curiosity, and destroying that implicit faith and security, which is the bane of all reasoning and free inquiry" (EHU IV (i), p. 26)

Indeed it is, and in all spheres. Yet there is every reason to believe that "moral subjects" are the worst afflicted by this bane. For these deal in the main with the intended and unintended results of intended human action. And, whilst most of us much of the time are inclined to believe that we already know what must be the results of acting in this way or in that, the fact is that "that implicit faith and security" is not only groundless but also, most often, substantially wrong. For in truth policies quite often produce results quite contrary to the intentions of their promoters, and always they carry other consequences which in fact no one foresaw or intended or perhaps could have foreseen or intended. Hume's own *History*, like all histories, is full of instances. Let us, however, on this occasion mention two extremely important contemporary examples in which the "reasoning and free inquiry" of first-rate social scientists has demonstrated that the actual effects of certain lavishly funded and enthusiastically implemented programmes have turned out to be flat contrary to the hopes and promises of their promoters. In both cases the full titles of the research reports give for our purposes sufficient indications of the nature and tenor of the findings. One, from the USA, is Charles Murray's *Losing Ground: American Social Policy, 1950-1980*; the other, by Alice Coleman and other members of the Design Disadvantagement Team at King's College, London, is *Utopia on Trial: Vision and Reality in Planned Housing*.

In the first *Enquiry* the most prominent purpose served by the conceptual scheme embodied in Hume's Fork is that of discrediting all but one of the traditional arguments of Natural Theology; and, as was indicated by the quotations at the end of the present section 3, the same methods are later employed in pursuit of the same purposes in the *Dialogues*. In the castrated *Treatise* there had been only a few hints of the shape of things to come. Nevertheless these were, in some readers of the spryer sort, sufficient to raise suspicions of infidelity. One of these hints is in the section 'Of the idea of existence, and of external existence', a section immediately following the discussions of the ideas of space and time. For Hume, finding that "the idea of existence is not deriv'd from any particular impression", concludes that it must be "the very same with the idea of what we conceive to be existent" (I (ii) 6, p. 66).

Whatever difficulties Hume should have had in accommodating such a simple idea without its single corresponding impression, the solution which he proposed clearly threatened the Ontological

Argument. "Being", as the second great philosopher of the Enlightenment was later to object, "is obviously not a real predicate; that is, it is not a concept of something which could be added to the concept of a thing" (Kant, 1781, p. 504). But now in the first *Enquiry* the appeal is to different principles, and it is not the Ontological Argument alone which is threatened. Instead all save the Argument to Design are involved in a common ruin; while that, as an argument from experience, is reserved for separate, more respectful, but equally devastating treatment.

The whole comprehensive dismissal comes within a single page as the book works up to its purple peroration: "Whatever *is* may *not be*. No negation of fact can involve a contradiction . . . that Caesar, or the angel Gabriel, or any being never existed, may be a false proposition, but still is perfectly conceivable and implies no contradiction." So much for the Ontological Argument. Now for all those others which presuppose that we can know apriori what things or sorts of things either must be or cannot be causes of other things or sorts of things: "The existence, therefore, of any being can only be proved by arguments from its cause or its effect; and these arguments are founded entirely on experience . . . It is only experience, which teaches us the nature and bounds of cause and effect, and enables us to infer the existence of one object from that of another" (EHU XII (iii), p. 164).

Finally we have perhaps the most quoted passage in all Hume's writings, the passage which led the old original Logical Positivists of the Vienna Circle to hail him as their spiritual father: "When we run over libraries, persuaded of these principles, what havoc must we make? If we take in our hand any volume – of divinity or school metaphysics, for instance – let us ask, *Does it contain any abstract reasoning concerning quantity or number?* No. *Does it contain any experimental reasoning concerning matter of fact and existence?* No. Commit it then to the flames, for it can contain nothing but sophistry and illusion" (ibid., p. 165).

# 4

# Argument from Experience, and the Religious Hypothesis

There was at one time some scholarly dispute as to whether Hume was better seen as a philosophical sceptic or a scientific naturalist. It is a question which never should have been argued, since the truth is manifest that he wanted always to be something of both. What may more reasonably be discussed is how far he ever succeeded in reconciling these two desires. Yet here too, although the question can be –and certainly has been – disputed, there must in the end be only one correct answer: "Hume could not succeed in the impossible – a science founded on scepticism no degree of ingenuity can successfully construct" (Passmore, 1952, p. 151).

The tension between scepticism and science is there right from the start. For even on its title page the *Treatise* is presented as a scientific project (p. xi). Yet the interlocking Cartesian assumptions from which he begins imply a nescience even more absolute than any which he himself suggests. The judgement of the *Abstract* is, therefore, abundantly justified: "The reader will easily perceive that the philosophy contain'd in this book is very sceptical, and tends to give us a notion of the imperfections and narrow limits of human understanding" (p. 657).

## 1 THE IRRECOVERABLY FAILED DEDUCTION

It was in Part I of Section IV of the first *Enquiry* that Hume developed a fundamental distinction: between stating, or purporting to state, the relations of ideas; and propositions stating, or purporting to state, matters of fact and real existence. In Part II he proceeded to employ this distinction, along with the first of his three Cartesian principles, in setting up what has since come to be called The Problem of Induction. It is a misleading description, in two ways. First, although Hume here is writing much more as the logician and much less as the psychologist than in the *Treatise*, he never in this context actually employs the word 'induction', but only the expression 'conclusions from experience'. Second, despite some ironic show of modesty, Hume clearly thinks he is offering a demonstration. We should be reminded of his remark made earlier in another connection: "that nothing can be more absurd, than this custom of calling a *difficulty* what pretends to be a *demonstration*, and endeavouring by that means to elude its force and evidence" (THN I (ii) 2, p. 31).

Hume's demonstration is a demonstration of the impossibility of deducing propositions of the form 'All X's have been, are and will be Φ' from propositions of the form 'All so far observed, or otherwise known X's are or have been Φ'. He thus sees all conclusions from experience as invalidly deduced, by a syllogism for which no adequate minor premise can be supplied: "When a man says, *I have found, in all past instances, such sensible qualities conjoined with such secret powers*, and when he says, *Similar sensible qualities will always be conjoined with similar secret powers*, he is not guilty of a tautology . . . You say that the one proposition is an inference from the other; but you must confess that the inference is not intuitive, neither is it demonstrative" (EHU IV (ii), p. 37).

If this really is a true representation of the form of argument from experience, then what we need is a known minor premise to complete a valid syllogism: "There is required", as Hume so nicely puts it, "a medium which may enable the mind to draw such an inference."He adds, darkly, "if indeed it be drawn by reasoning and argument" (ibid., p. 34). Yet where is this medium, that is middle term, to be found? Hume continues: "That there are no demonstrative arguments in the case seems evident; since it implies no contradiction that the course of nature may change, and that an object, seemingly like those we have experienced, may be attended with different or contrary effects." The alternative is one of the sort which "regard matter of fact and real existence . . . But . . . we have said that all arguments concerning existence are founded on the relation of cause and effect; that our knowledge of that relation is derived entirely from experience; and that all our experimental conclusions proceed on the supposition that the future will be conformable to the past." So to try to prove that very supposition in this way "must evidently be going in a circle, and taking that for granted which is the very point in question" (pp. 35 and 36).

It is well, in order fully to grasp the nature and force of Hume's demonstration, first to write down the major premise and the desired conclusion, and then to pencil in one or two possible candidates for the minor premise vacancy. A first suggestion is: 'All x's have been or are known or observed.' This certainly will yield a sound syllogism. But it does so only at the cost of disqualifying the result as a faithful representation of the nerve of argument from experience. What it gives us is an analysis of the features of the experience already available; not an account of how we do, or should, use the already known or observed as a guide to the character of what is not yet, and perhaps may never be, directly known or observed.

By the way: the so-called Problem of Induction is often set as a problem only of moves from present and past to future. But Hume himself does not restrict it in this way. His "historical projects" ensured that he would be equally, and equally rightly, concerned about moves from data about the present and past to conclusions about the not directly known past (Klibansky and Mossner, 1954, p. 23). Thus he says in the first part of the same Section IV: "A man finding a watch or any other machine in a desert island would conclude that there had once been men in that island" (EHU IV (i), p. 26. A similar passage in Section XI referring to "seeing upon the sea-shore the print of one human foot" constitutes an even stronger reminder that Daniel Defoe had published *Robinson Crusoe* in 1719!)

An alternative suggestion for filling the vacant slot in the syllogism is: 'The class of all X's so far known or observed, is in all respects a perfect sample of the class of all X's.' This has two merits: first, it yields a valid syllogism; and, second, it yields a syllogism which is at any rate not quite obviously untrue to the nature of argument from experience. It is, in fact, a more precise, detemporalized formulation of the proposition considered by Hume himself: "that the future will be conformable to the past."

That proposition, however, as Hume insisted, cannot serve; since it could itself only be known as a conclusion from experience. But the situation is in truth worse than this. For, once Hume's proposition has been given the more precise formulation required in order to enable it to serve as the minor premise of a valid syllogism, it becomes clear that, even without appeal to the particular form of argument in question, it can be and surely is known by everyone to be false. For all of us have discovered at some time that, whereas all the members previously known to us from some class were Φ, at least one other newly noticed member of that same class is, after all, not Φ.

Once the case has been thus clearly and compellingly put, everything becomes obvious. Of course, universal conclusions about matters of fact cannot be validly deduced from less than universal premises of the same sort. For is not a valid deductive argument defined as one in which it is impossible without self-contradiction simultaneously to assert the premises and to deny the conclusion? But, this said, we have then to insist that obviousness really is, what so many other things nowadays are falsely said to be, essentially relative. So such present obviousness neither necessarily nor in fact sustains any derogation from Hume's philosophical genius (Price, 1940b). And, furthermore, even if it is now obvious that Hume produced a demonstration, it still remains very far from obvious what morals we ought to draw.

## 2 WHAT MORAL DOES HUME'S DEMONSTRATION POINT?

"And although none but a fool or madman will ever pretend to dispute the authority of experience, or to reject that great guide of human life" (EHU IV (ii), p. 36), Hume nevertheless entitles his immediately subsequent Section V 'Sceptical solution of these doubts'. This sceptical solution is "that, in all reasonings from experience, there is a step taken by the mind which is not supported by any argument or process of the understanding . . ." But "If the mind be not engaged by argument to make this step, it must be induced by some other principle of equal weight and authority . . . This principle is Custom or Habit. For wherever the repetition of any particular act or operation produces a propensity to renew the same act or operation, without being impelled by any reasoning or process of the understanding, we always say, that this propensity is the effect of Custom." This is "a principle of human nature, which is universally acknowledged" (V (i), pp. 41 and 43).

It is, as Hume is eager to stress, a principle of the nature also of the brutes – animals other than man. For these, "as well as men, learn many things from experience . . . It is impossible that this inference of the animal can be founded on any process of argument or reasoning . . . It is custom alone, which engages animals, from every object which strikes their senses, to infer its usual attendant . . ." (IX, pp. 105 and 106). "All inferences from experience, therefore, are effects of custom; not of reasoning" (V (i), p. 43).

Hume's own "sceptical solution" involves a subtle and, as it is actually presented, questionable shift from one universe of discourse to another. Starting from an enquiry into the logical nature and status of arguments from experience, Hume slides across into discussing the psychology of learning. This move, which does not of course present itself to him in quite this light, is apparently mediated by the assumption that only a conclusion either resulting from or supported by reasoning can be reasonable. Thus he makes much of the fact "that the most ignorant and stupid peasants, nay infants, nay even brute beasts" are able to learn from experience, although quite incapable of offering reasons adequate to justify the step of supposing "the past resembling the future" (IV (ii), p. 39). Yet it is entirely possible for it to be reasonable to do something without the agent being aware of, or even capable of appreciating, the good reasons which could be deployed in support.

There are two extra points about rationality which have to be made at once. First that, since no chain of justification can be without end, it is always possible and sometimes necessary for something to be reasonable notwithstanding that there is no room for any further supporting reasons. Second, it appears that Hume is here relying on the second clause of what in section 2 of chapter 1 we distinguished as the first of three interlocking Cartesian assumptions: "that no knowledge claim can be adequately vindicated by offering an evidencing reason for belief which does not actually entail the truth of the proposition asserted as known." It is an assumption which consists ill with the promise of the *Abstract* to supply the defect of philosophers "who are very copious when they explain the operations of the understanding in the form of demonstrations, but are too concise when they treat of probabilities" (pp. 646-7). For what, after all, is probabilifying evidence if it is not some reason for believing which nevertheless does not entail the truth of the proposition thus evidenced (Stove, 1973)?

After contending that argument from experience engages the principle of custom or habit rather than that of reason, Hume proceeds without any signs of embarrassment, to insist that it is, after all, paradigmatically reasonable to allow experience to be our guide to belief about matters of fact. "A wise man," he insists, as he starts to discuss miracles, "proportions his belief to the evidence" (X (i), p. 110). Again, in the following Section XI, it is to argument from experience that those who would "establish religion upon the principles of reason" most rightly propose to appeal (p. 135). And so on. All this is in itself, of course, well and fine. But it simply cannot be made to consist with Hume's 'Sceptical doubts concerning the operations of the understanding'. Nor will it do, as has in our time sometimes been done, to maintain, while leaving his account unchallenged, that deduction and induction are just different forms of equally legitimate argument, each with its own different yet equally proper canons. That contention too may in itself be all very well. But if the form of inductive argument really is what Hume represented it to be, then it is different from deduction only in as much as it must be always and necessarily invalid.

In order to bring out more clearly the true implications of what Popper hails as Hume's refutation of induction, it may help to notice Popper's own consequent rash rejections both of the idea of actual scientific knowledge and of the putative heresy of 'justificationism'. He says in *The Logic of Scientific Discovery* – and, so far as I know, he has never either withdrawn or adequately qualified these assertions – that "The old scientific idea of *episteme* – of absolutely certain, demonstrable knowledge – has proved to be an idol . . . every scientific statement must remain tentative for *ever* . . . The wrong view of science betrays itself in the craving to be right; for it is not his *possession* of knowledge of irrefutable truth, that makes the man of science, but his recklessly critical *quest* for truth." Again, later, he explains that "We must not look upon science as a 'body of knowledge', but rather as a system of hypotheses . . . a system of guesses . . . of which we are never justified in saying that we know that they are 'true' or 'more or less certain' or even 'probable'" (Popper, 1934, pp. 280-1 and 337).

Even if we are intended to apply these claims only to universal propositions or to some sub-class thereof, the claims must still be put down as manifestations of a most extreme and intolerably paradoxical sort of scepticism (Stove, 1982). The reason, surely, why Popper becomes committed to them is that he has accepted: both Hume's account of "conclusions from experience"; and the first if not so clearly also the second of our three Cartesian principles? (We shall discover later that he also, perhaps more surprisingly, accepts the third.)

Certainly, if I know, then I cannot be wrong; in the sense that from 'I know p' it follows necessarily that p is true. But it would not follow from that premise that I am or was, even in some one restricted area of assertion, infallible. Nor, since the argument is invalid, can we reverse it; concluding, from the premise that I am not infallible, and hence always conceivably could be mistaken, that I can indeed never know anything.

It is equally wrong to hold that Hume's "refutation of induction" justifies a rejection of 'justificationism'; justifies us, that is to say, in maintaining that there can never be sufficient, or perhaps any, evidencing reason for holding that any "hypotheses . . . are 'true' or 'more or less certain' or even 'probable'." For that "refutation"itself takes for granted exactly what is in dispute – whether any cognitive claim can be adequately vindicated by offering any evidencing reason for belief which does not actually entail the truth of the proposition thus evidenced. It takes this for granted by accepting the representation of all argument from experience as involving an irreparably ill-starred attempt to deduce an universal conclusion from some less than universal premise. In his own way Hume puts this point himself in the first *Enquiry*: "If we be, therefore, engaged by arguments to put trust in past experience, and make it the standard of our future judgement, these arguments must be probable only, or such as regard matter of fact and real existence, according to the division above mentioned. But that there is no argument of this kind, must appear, if our explication of that species of reasoning be admitted as solid and satisfactory" (IV (ii), p. 35). If that is indeed admitted then surely it must so appear!

If we now start to seek a more satisfactory account of the fundamental form of all such argument we shall discover that, as so often, Hume supplies us with some hints for his own correction. Thus he finds it natural to speak not of the assumption but of "the presumption of a resemblance betwixt those objects, of which we have had experience, and those, of which have had none" (THN I (iii) 6, p. 90; and compare p. 91). On other occasions, while again eschewing the word 'assumption', he prefers to write: "We are determined by CUSTOM alone to suppose the future conformable to the past"

(*Abstract*, p. 652; and compare EHU IV (ii), p. 35). Yet again, Hume as the student of human nature notices how and what "we always presume", and that "If a body of like colour and consistency with that bread, which we have formerly eat, be presented to us, we make no scruple of repeating the experiment, and foresee, with certainty, like nourishment and support" (ibid., p. 33).

We should also compare what Newton said in the 'Rules of Reasoning in Philosophy', rules which preface Book III of the *Principia*. Hume was certainly familiar with these rules, accepting and admiring Newton as one of what would nowadays be rated his own role models (Capaldi, 1975). Yet Newton had nothing to say about deducing "conclusions from experience", or about some supposed need to assume the Uniformity of Nature. Instead his third rule runs: "The qualities of bodies . . . which are found to belong to all bodies within reach of our experiments, are to be esteemed the universal qualities of all bodies whatsoever." The fourth, which "we must follow, that the argument of induction may not be evaded by arbitrary hypotheses", states: "In experimental philosophy we are to look upon propositions inferred by general induction from phenomena as accurately or very nearly true . . . till such time as other phenomena occur, by which they may either be made more accurate, or liable to exceptions" (Newton, 1686, pp. 398-400).

These hints should together suggest that it is neither necessary nor correct to represent the form of all arguments from experience as a broken-backed syllogism, crippled for lack of a suitable second premise. The much talked of yet rather rarely formulated Principle of Induction, upon which all conclusions from experience are sometimes supposed somehow to depend, might instead be offered: not as the indispensable, hidden and ultimately indefensible missing premise which completes and validates all such supposed syllogisms; but as a rational rule of procedure to guide us in shaping always fallible and corrigible expectations in which to approach the unknown. This rule in its most elementary form would be something like: 'Where and so long as all known X's are or have been $\Phi$, to presume that all X's have been are and will be $\Phi$, until and unless some positive reason is found for revising this particular presumption.'

Since this is a rule for procedure rather than an assertion of alleged fact, no question arises of how, if at all, it could be known to be true. It is also the least dogmatic of rules, inasmuch as it contains within itself a provision for revising any resulting presumptions as and when these turn out to have been defeated. Such an insistence upon corrigibility can be constructively seen as a desired trophy of Hume's own philosophical investigations: "They may even prove useful, by exciting curiosity, and destroying that implicit faith and security which is the bane of all reasoning and free enquiry" (EHU IV (i), p. 26).

The questions which properly can arise about such a rule of procedure concern either the reasonableness and/or the results of its adoption. Yet, if and in so far as such a rule epitomizes the principle of all argument from experience, then to follow it must be as paradigmatically reasonable as to try to learn from experience. To challenge its reasonableness is, therefore, to challenge the established paradigm.

Hume, however, both as a practical person and as a moral scientist, expresses wholehearted agreement with that particular establishment: for "none but a fool or a madman will ever pretend to dispute the authority of experience, or to reject that great guide to human life . . ." (EHU IV (ii), p. 36). It is at this stage that we can find a place for Hume's appeals to the psychological principles of custom and instinct. For it could well be argued that any substantially different rules for procedure, which might be proposed as alternatives, would be so alien to the fundamentals of our human nature as to be totally impractical: we simply could not, for instance, obey the contrary rule of always presuming that the unknown will turn out to be opposite to the known (Flew, 1961, pp. 82ff.).

In thus finding a place, albeit, surely, a different place for Hume's psychological interests, we become enabled, as he would wish, to see man as a part of nature, and human learning as involving – as well as a whole lot else – the same fundamental psychological principles as all other animal learning. Attempts thus to connect human with animal psychology are typical. There are three whole sections in the *Treatise* and one in the first *Enquiry* in which, after considering some aspect of human nature, Hume turns to look how far the same ideas can be applied to the brutes. In seeing learning as thus grounded in basic biological dispositions Hume sometimes seems to have been tempted to romanticize the "wisdom of nature" in securing "so necessary an act of the mind by some instinct or mechanical tendency." Yet never-sleeping academic scepticism is there to add: "which *may* be infallible in its operations" (EHU V (ii), p. 55: italics supplied).

## 3 ONE NOBLER PART RESTORED

Fully to appreciate Sections X and XI of the first *Enquiry* you have to know: both that they constitute a complementary pair; and that the establishment of what they are together intended to establish is crucial to the whole project. These things need to be said, and emphasized. They have often been neglected, or even denied. Thus in the nineteenth century, in the printing in Sir John Lubbock's Hundred Books series, both sections were excised – to be relegated to a kind of appendix, introduced by a note beginning: "These essays are generally omitted in popular editions of the writings of Hume." As late as 1893, in the Introduction to the original Clarendon edition, Selby-Bigge maintained that "Their insertion . . . is due doubtless to other considerations than . . . a simple desire to illustrate or draw corollaries from the philosophical principles laid down [in the *Treatise*]" (p. xix). It seems never to have occurred to him to ask what the purposes of the first *Enquiry* were, or to attend to Hume's own answer, sharply stated in Section I. They were, of course: in general, to draw the limits of the human understanding; and, in particular, to provide in so doing a prophylactic against "religious fears and prejudices" (p. 11).

In order to fulfil this corollary purpose Hume had to justify an aggressive agnosticism: not just a feeble confession of individual unknowing; but instead a strong claim that positive knowledge must be, in this area, impossible. Hume's strong claim was, nevertheless, weaker than the characteristic contention of those neo-Humian successors, the Logical Positivists: they maintained that any talk about a transcendent God must be not merely false or evidentially unwarranted but altogether 'without literal significance'. There are perhaps hints of some similar view in the final *Dialogues*; suggestions that, after all the necessary qualifications have been made on both sides, disputes in this area may come to have a vanishingly small factual content. But in these two sections Hume is raising epistemological rather than semantic questions. And his method is to demolish the most powerful case for the contrary conclusion that religious knowledge is possible.

That most powerful case was in his day developed in two stages. In the first the enquirer was presented with arguments of natural reason; (natural reason being contrasted with divine revelation). These arguments, of which by far the most popularly persuasive was, and is, the Argument to Design, were supposed to provide or to prove a Natural Theology. Then, in a second stage, the resulting somewhat sketchy religion of nature was to be supplemented by a richer Revelation. Since, however, there had been, have been and no doubt will continue to be many candidates claiming to be the uniquely true Revelation, the Christian candidate had, and has, somehow to be shown to be that one authentic claimant. The preferred method was to maintain that there is sufficient historical evidence to prove the occurrence of both the constitutive and the endorsing miracles of Christianity. (Miracles must be endorsements since they would necessarily involve an overriding of a law of Nature; which could be brought about only by Supernature.)

Anyone who wants to know more about the controversial background is referred to Leslie Stephen's classic *History of English Thought in the Eighteenth Century.* Anyone who, knowing that this or indeed any other kind of rational apologetic has in some still professedly Christian circles gone right out of fashion, draws the conclusion that all the controversies should have been forgotten long since, needs to be reminded that the possibilities of completing both stages were defined as essential dogmata of the Roman Catholic faith by what has now become the First Vatican Council of 1870-1 (Denzinger, 1953, §§ 1806 and 1813).

Section X 'Of miracles' opens with a transparently mischievous tribute to the late Latitudinarian Archbishop Tillotson, and ends with two memorable mordant, fiercely derisive sentences. But Section XI, given the misleading and seemingly innocuous title 'Of a particular providence and of a future state', is represented cautiously as the gist of a "conversation with a friend who loves sceptical paradoxes; where, though he advanced many principles, of which I can by no means approve, yet, as they seem to be curious and to bear some relation to the chain of reasoning carried on throughout this enquiry, I shall here copy them from my memory as accurately as I can, in order to submit them to the judgement of the reader" (p. 132).

In this caution Hume was wise after his own generation. For, whereas in the first of these two sections he was attacking openly and directly in an area where Deist writers had been sniping for a long time, in the second he was sapping to undermine a formerly unchallenged citadel. Thus *The Analogy of Religion,* the classic contemporary reply to the Deists, simply assumed that the Argument to

Design was unthreatened and undisputed common ground: "There is no need of abstruse reasonings and distinctions, to convince an unprejudiced understanding, that there is a God who made and governs the world, and will judge it in righteousness . . . to an unprejudiced mind ten thousand thousand instances of design cannot but prove a designer" (Butler, 1896, II (ix) 2; vol. I, p. 371).

We should, therefore, not be surprised to find Hume wrapping up his subversive suggestions so carefully that many readers fail to appreciate their revolutionary significance. Anyone wanting to follow the process of unwrapping through in detail is referred to Flew, 1961, chapter IX. But for the rest of us the next step is to explain what Hume was arguing against. This has come to be called the Argument *from* Design. But it is more apt, especially in the present context, to speak of an or the Argument *to* Design. For the former expression would be appropriate to a deductive argument spelling out the relations of ideas; an argument proceeding from a question-begging premise stating that the Universe is a designed artefact to the unsurprising and already implicit conclusion that it must be the work of some Universe-Maker. But, as Hume is all the time insisting, arguments of this sort are altogether unsuitable for establishing "matters of fact and real existence". Such "conclusions from experience" could only be sustained by an Argument *to* Design. This has to proceed: from features of the Universe which, experience suggests, could only have come about as a result of design: to the conclusion that the whole is indeed the work of a Great Designer.

This argument, happily described as "the religious hypothesis" is, in the mouths of Hume's opponents, said to be "derived from the order of nature; where there appear such marks of intelligence and design, that you think it extravagant to assign for its cause, either chance, or the blind and unguided force of matter. You allow, that this is an argument drawn from effects to causes. From the order of the work, you infer, that there must have been project and forethought in the workman. If you cannot make out this point, you allow that your conclusion fails; and you pretend not to establish the conclusion with a greater latitude than the phenomena of nature will justify" (pp. 146 and 135-6).

Hume's first counter-move is as simple as it is brilliant, and devastating in its implications. Indeed it ought to be emphasized that the brilliance and elegance of his work in this area is such that those who in their general discussions of his philosophy neglect it do most serious injustice to his total achievement. Hume says, very quietly: "If the cause be known only by the effect, we never ought to ascribe to it any qualities, beyond what are precisely requisite to produce the effect: Nor can we by any rules of just reasoning return back from the cause, and infer other effects from it, beyond those by which alone it is known to us" (p. 136).

That is, of course, obvious. However, like so many other truths which become obvious once they have been firmly stated, this Humian truism carries important implications. It is to these that the argument proceeds: "Allowing, therefore, the gods to be the authors of the existence or order of the universe; it follows, that they possess that precise degree of power, intelligence, and benevolence, which appears in their workmanship; but nothing farther can ever be proved, except as we call in the assistance of exaggeration and flattery to supply the defects of argument and reasoning" (p. 137).

This call is in fact made whenever anyone tries to pull the God of Abraham, Isaac and Israel out of the hat labelled 'Argument to Design'. For the power and the knowledge minimally required to produce the Universe must, though very vast, fall far short of Omnipotence and Omniscience. So evidences of design can, at most and by themselves, point only to a different god, and one much smaller than that of mainstream traditional theism. With such evaluative characteristics as goodness or perfection things are, if anything, even worse. For here the case is, not that the evidence is insufficient to warrant, but that it appears actually to refute, the drastic conclusions desired. The theists' Problem of Evil precisely is their apparently insoluble problem of reconciling many undenied and undeniable facts about the Universe as we know it with the supposedly complementary Divine characteristics of infinite power and infinite goodness. These are attributed arbitrarily to a Being postulated to explain the origin and continuation of a Universe manifestly much less than perfect. The problem, of course, is not a problem at all for those refusing to make any of these misguided moves.

Hume's second counter-move – which, borrowing the phrase from Berkeley, he might have claimed to be "the killing blow" – is one of the most elegant things in all his writings. This elegance is deeply concealed behind veils of discreet precaution. It consists in bringing out that the Argument to Design, as an argument from experience, can find no purchase here, since in this limiting case both the putative Cause and the alleged Effect are by definition unique.

Any critic of the Argument to Design has to meet a challenge: "If you saw, for instance, a half-finished building, surrounded with heaps of brick and stone and mortar, and all the instruments of masonry; could you not *infer* from the effect, that it was the work of design and contrivance? . . . Why then do you refuse to admit the same method of reasoning with regard to the order of nature?" (p. 143). Upon what grounds, the challenger asks, is the claim to a parity of reasoning rejected? Surely it could be as legitimate to frame some hypothesis about a god, and to attempt with its aid to explain and predict further phenomena, as it is to postulate the existence of atoms, and to try to explain and predict in terms of the attributes ascribed to these similarly invisible entities?

The crucial difference, Hume answers, lies in "The infinite difference of the subjects . . ." (p. 143). In the first place, "The Deity is known to us only by his productions, and is a single being . . ., not comprehended under any species or genus, from whose experienced attributes or qualities we can, by analogy, infer any attribute or quality in him" (p. 144). In the second place, the Universe itself, in the sense of everything there is (with the exception of the Deity, if such there be) is also by definition both unique and the provider of all the experience ever available to us.

Hume is, in the first count, drawing out – with the simplicity of genius – a necessary but unnoticed consequence of the accepted defining characteristics of the theist God. For, in *The Analogy of Religion*, we read: "Upon supposition that God exercises a moral government over the world, the analogy of this natural government suggests and makes it credible that this moral government must be a scheme, quite beyond our comprehension: and this affords a general answer to all objections against the justice and goodness of it" (Butler, 1736, I (vii) 3; vol. I, p. 161).

It helps to compare and contrast the entirely different case of a straightforwardly finite and anthropomorphic god, conjured up in an attempt to account for some but not all the phenomena of the Universe. Let us postulate, for instance, a sea-god Poseidon, with the familiar attributes of arbitrary human despots; deduce that he will protect his votaries and afflict those who defy him; and then organize some experiments to test our hypothesis. Members of the experimental group are asked to make vows to Poseidon, promising to erect grateful commemorative tablets and other votive offerings if they are returned home safely from their voyages; while the members of the control group are required to express incredulity about the existence of Poseidon, or otherwise to blaspheme against Poseidon's name. Certainly we have here a religious hypothesis of a sort, and certainly it is respectably testable. But of course this is not at all what Hume meant by "the religious hypothesis"; nor yet what his opponents, the theist Natural Theologians, are supposed to have in mind. There is a world of difference between any such hypothetical god and God.

On the second count, although there is a regrettable sense in which the Andromeda Nebula might be spoken of as 'an island universe', the Universe whose existence and regularities "the religious hypothesis" might be thought to explain is by definition the only one of its kind. But this second essential uniqueness too carries its own restrictive consequence. However far back we may be able to trace the – so to speak – internal history of the Universe, there can be no question of arguing that this or that external origin is either probable or improbable. We do not have, and we necessarily could not have, experience of other Universes to show or suggest that Universes, or Universes with these particular features, are the work of Gods, or of Gods of this or that particular sort. To improve slightly on a famous remark by C. S. Peirce: 'Universes, unlike universes, are not as plentiful as blackberries.'

It may help here to imagine some more-than-Methuselah in a space ship, approaching some still unexplored 'island universe'. He might well, to the exasperated distress of his younger colleagues, refer to the wealth of his experience: 'Mark my words. Man and boy these million million years I have . . .'; and so on, and no doubt on and on and on. But the unique Universe is and must be itself all we have. How it is, is just how it is; and that's that.

Hume brings it all together in what he pretends is an awkward and embarrassing afterthought: "It is only when two *Species* of objects are found to be constantly conjoined, that we can infer the one from the other . . . If experience and observation and analogy be, indeed, the only guides which we can reasonably follow in inferences of this nature; both the effect and cause must bear a similarity . . . to other effects and causes, which we know, and which we have found, in many instances, to be conjoined with each other. I leave it to your own reflection to pursue the consequences of this principle" (p. 148).

Presumably this paragraph provided one of the stimuli which awoke Kant from his "dogmatic slumbers"; and his reflections thereon led in *A Critique of Pure Reason* to the wholly Humian conclusion that we cannot apply the concepts of cause and effect outwith the limits of our experience. Hume's own further reflections are pursued in the *Dialogues* – "in all respects [his] maturest work . . . beyond any question the greatest work on philosophy of religion in the English language" (Penelhum, 1975, p. 171. One of the most perverse judgements in what has some claim to have been the worst work ever written about Hume comes at p. 150 of Basson, 1958: "Hume produced no serious philosophical writings after the *Enquiries*").

Since the *Dialogues* are indeed dialogues, very scrupulously composed on the model particularly of Cicero's *de Natura Deorum*, it is no more possible to deduce Hume's personal position directly from this text than we can deduce Shakespeare's political and religious convictions from his plays. But in Hume's case we have sufficient biographical evidence for it to be a tolerably safe bet that it was what, following Bayle, Hume called Stratonician atheism. (Strato of Lampsacus was next but one in succession to Aristotle as Head of the Lyceum.) If this conjecture is correct, then the final conviction of the author of the *Dialogues* was that we have to accept as ultimate the existence of the Universe and the subsistence of whatever our scientists find to be its most fundamental laws.

To appreciate the strength of such a position, we need to be seized of the point that every system of explanation must include at least some fundamentals which are not themselves explained. However far you rise in an hierarchy of explanations – particular events in terms of general laws, laws in terms of theories, theories in terms of wider and more comprehensive theories, and maybe even further – still there has to be at every stage, including the last stage, some element, or some elements, in terms of which whatever is explained at that stage is explained. Nor is this inevitability of logic escaped by the theist. For whatever else he may think to explain by reference to the existence and nature of his God, he cannot thereby avoid taking that existence and that nature as itself ultimate and beyond explanation.

This necessity is common to all systems. It is no fault in any, and certainly not a competitive weakness. The Principle of Sufficient

Reason – that there has to be a sufficient reason for anything and everything being as it is, was, and will be – is not, as has often been thought, necessarily true. It is, instead, demonstrably false (Penelhum, 1960). Granted this insight, how can we fail to see that there is no possible explanatory point in hypothesizing a Cause to which all and only those powers and inclinations necessary and sufficient to guarantee the production of the Universe as it is, are then gratuitously attributed? In what are always said to have been the words of William of Ockham: "Entities are not to be multiplied beyond necessity."

# 5

## The Necessity of Causes,
## and the Impossibility of the Miraculous

We have already heard Hume insist that "The contrary of every matter of fact is still possible; because it can never imply a contradiction, and is conceived by the mind with the same facility and distinctness, as if ever so conformable to reality" (EHU IV (i), p. 25). We cannot, therefore, save by appealing to experience, discover any limitations upon what sort of thing may or may not be the cause of what, or what sort of cause might or might not be required by what. As is so often the case, the significance and the importance of this contention comes out best when we consider what it commits its supporters to rejecting. In the *Treatise*, for instance, Hume applies it to destroy the argument that changes in consciousness – changes in "thought or perception" – could not possibly result from the motions of merely material atoms (I (iv) 5, pp. 246-7).

Nevertheless it seems that, while composing "that juvenile work", he failed to notice that his principles required him to challenge the claim, urged by Newton among others, that action at a distance is inconceivable. (Compare the Third Letter to Bentley, quoted by Burtt, 1932, pp. 265–6.) Certainly Hume does in Book I say that causes must be contiguous with their effects, both in space and in time (THN I (iii) 2, pp. 75-6). But this stipulation is abandoned in the first *Enquiry*. More important, he was by then emboldened to invade the territories of Natural Theology and, "persuaded of these principles", to make havoc there (XII (iii), p. 165).

One of the items of "divinity or school metaphysics" which Hume must have had in mind was the "Arguments demonstrating the existence of God . . . drawn up in geometrical fashion", which Descartes had appended to his reply to the second set of Objections to the *Meditations*. There the four theorems of the theological geometry are preceded by a list of ten "Axioms or Common Principles". The fourth is: "Whatever reality or perfection exists in a thing , exists formally or eminently in its first and adequate cause." The eighth runs: "That which can effect what is greater or more difficult, can also accomplish what is less." It is to these and similar principles – which to him seemed not merely true but self-evidently, indeed necessarily, true – that Descartes appeals in his attempts to demonstrate: that "this idea of God, which exists in us, must have God as its cause"; and that "if I had the power of conserving my own existence, I should have had a . . . power of giving myself the perfections that I lack . . . I do not have . . . Therefore I do not have the power of conserving myself . . . Consequently it is another being that conserves my existence" (Descartes, 1642, II pp. 52, 56, 57 and 58).

In the *Treatise*, after disposing of all such more particular axioms, Hume goes on to tackle the most general causal "maxim . . . that *whatever begins to exist must have a cause of existence*" (I (iii) 3, p. 78). He disposes in a very brisk way of contentions rather vaguely attributed to Hobbes, Locke, Clarke and others (MacNabb and Khamara, 1977). For the contradictory of this most general maxim too is conceivable, involves no contradiction: just as there can be bachelors although every husband must have a wife, so there might conceivably be bachelor events though every effect must have a cause.

Since the claim that every event has a cause is not the sort of thing which can be known apriori, "that opinion must necessarily arise from observation and experience." Hume never tells us just how this is supposed to happen, preferring "to sink this question in the following, *Why we conclude, that such particular causes must necessarily have such particular effects, and why we form an inference from one to another?*" (THN I (iii) 3, p. 82). Kemp Smith suggested that in "that opinion" we had another example of unevidenced yet irresistible natural belief, like the belief in the existence of body. But this case is different, since it is, apparently, a belief which "the vulgar", holding to the reality of uncaused chance occurrences, do not always share. Certainly there are abundant indications in Hume's published works, as well as an outright affirmation in a letter (Greig, 1932, I, p. 187), that he had no intention of denying something so "commonly allow'd by philosophers" (THN I (iii), 12, p. 130. For similarities and dissimilarities between the positions of Hume and of Kant compare Kuehn, 1979 and 1983.)

## 1 HOW CAUSES ARE NECESSARY

But now, if it is not necessarily true – not, that is, a truth the contradictory of which is self-contradictory – either that certain sorts of things must have certain sorts of causes or that every event must have some sort of cause, the questions arise: "Why we conclude that such particular causes must *necessarily* have such particular effects?" (THN I (iii) 2, p. 78); and "*What is our idea of necessity, when we say that two objects are necessarily connected together?*" (I (iii) 14, p. 155). Since he holds it "more probable, that these expressions do here lose their true meaning by being *wrong apply'd*, than that they never have any meaning" (ibid., p. 162), Hume becomes committed to searching for the parent impression.

Restricted as he is by his Cartesian presuppositions, Hume cannot discover the source of this idea in his experience of the occurrence of 'objects' of one sort causing the occurrence of 'objects' of another sort. "It must, therefore, be deriv'd from some internal impression, or impression of reflection." The conclusion then seems inescapable: "Either we have no idea of necessity, or necessity is nothing but that determination of the thought to pass from causes to effects and from effects to causes, according to their experienc'd union" (THN I (iii) 14, pp. 166 and 167). However, for Hume this is not just a conclusion which has to be accepted humbly, even if reluctantly. Instead it appears to him as a triumph of the hoped-for new science of man. For his account makes it seem that causal necessity is really in the mind of the observer and not, as the uninstructed laity would have it, in whatever 'objects' are said to be causally related.

Not causal necessity only but, as he will soon go on to argue, all evaluative characteristics also, are thus secondary rather than primary qualities. This distinction has had a long history, going back at least as far as the Classical Greek atomists. Its core is a contrast: between, on the one hand, those qualities (called primary) which things are supposed truly to possess 'in themselves'; and, on the other hand, those other only so-called qualities (termed secondary) which allegedly amount to no more than reactions in us caused by other and primary characteristics. We all naturally project these secondary qualities out onto objects which, science teaches us, actually possess only primary qualities.

Since all this was among the commonplaces of the new science – what Hume calls the "modern philosophy" – he was bound to see it as constituting confirmation of his own discoveries: these were, as it were, more of the same. Whether directly or indirectly, he must have known of a famous passage in the *Opticks*: "For the Rays, to speak properly, are not coloured. In them there is nothing else than a certain Power and Disposition to stir up a Sensation of this or that Colour . . . in the Rays they are nothing but their Dispositions to propagate this or that Motion into the Sensorium, and in the Sensorium they are Sensations of those Motions under the Forms of Colour" (Newton, 1704, pp. 125-6: the word 'sensorium' is roughly equivalent to 'mind').

In the *Abstract* Hume pointed to his account of the origin and projection of the idea of necessary connection as one of the trophies of his employment of the "principle of the association of ideas". As the three basic principles of this association "are the only ties of our thoughts, they are really *to us* the cement of the universe, and all the operations of the mind must, in great measure, depend on them" (pp. 661 and 662; and compare Mackie, 1974). But, though Hume's psychological intentions must never be forgotten, these are not our concern here.

Having shown that there cannot be logically necessary connections between events, he searches for the source of the misconception, and suggests that it is due to the projection of an idea of psychological necessity. This is a curious explanation. Once, but only once, he comes near to suggesting that really there only is psychological necessity: "the necessity which makes two times two equal four, or three angles of a triangle equal to two right ones, lies only in the act of the understanding by which we consider and compare these ideas" (I (iii) 14, p. 166). Such a heroic move would be consistent with a radically psychological interpretation of the notion of relations of ideas. But it is not typical of the *Treatise*, and finds no place in the generally less psychological atmosphere of the first *Enquiry*.

There are, however, ways – ways never noticed by Hume – in which logical necessities, which properly characterize either propositions or the logical relations between propositions, do get fallaciously projected out onto the non-linguistic world of mind-independent objects. Attempts to deduce hard determinist conclusions from premises either containing no idea of necessity at all or else themselves possessing only the logical necessity of the tautological have been discussed by philosophers since at least the time of Aristotle; who himself presented the famous Problem of the Sea-fight in *de Interpretatione*, chapter IX. For us the simplest example is provided by the theme song beginning, "Che sarà, sarà. Whatever will be will be", and concluding that there is never anything which anyone can do to stop anything – the thesis of hard determinism.

In the interpretation in which it is true, indeed necessarily and tautologically true, the premise here says no more than that, for all values of X, from *X will be* it follows necessarily that *X will be*. Indeed it does, since, for any value of X, it must be self-contradictory simultaneously both to assert and to deny that *X will be*. Once all this is recognized it becomes quite obviously preposterous to try to derive from so nugatory a premise the formidably substantial conclusion that, in a hard determinist interpretation, *Whatever will be will be*.

To put the same point in another and more immediately relevant way, from *X will be* it does indeed follow necessarily, if somewhat unexcitingly, that *X will be*. What does not follow at all is that *X will necessarily be*. It simply does not follow, however we propose to construe the 'necessarily' thus illicitly intruded into the proposed conclusion. It does not follow, if it is to be taken as an indication that that proposition is itself necessarily and tautologically true. Nor does it follow, if it is to be alternatively construed as expressing the claim that to prevent the occurrence of X is physically impossible.

As always, once the nerve of a fallacy has been plainly exposed, it becomes hard to believe that any even halfway competent people could make such a mistake. Yet obviousness is – as has been stressed before – essentially relative. So in fact it has not been only the weakest philosophers who have made very heavy weather of such puzzles as the Problem of the Sea-fight. Outside philosophy, where the premises and the conclusions are likely to be both more particular and more exciting, it is easier still thus fallaciously to project logical necessities out onto the non-linguistic world of mind-independent objects.

Hume however, as again was said earlier, notwithstanding that his overriding concern was to deny logically necessary connections between objects, seems never to have recognized projections of the present sort. What he was concerned to deny is nicely summed up in the following definition: "A cause is such a reason, so that if we had a sufficiently comprehensive knowledge of what really takes place, we should see how and why the effect follows from the cause with logical necessity" (Stout, 1950, p. 1). Hume's own story "of what really takes place" involves a projection of a sort of psychological necessity, a felt "determination of the mind". This story he epitomizes in two so-called definitions. The fact that, without alleging any ambiguity in the word 'cause', he offers not one but two, which are manifestly not equivalent, should have, but has not always, alerted his critics (Beauchamp and Rosenberg, 1981, ch. 1; and compare Robinson, 1962). As later in his treatment of moral judgement, what Hume is offering is: not a descriptive definition of a word; but an account of what goes on when we employ that word correctly.

The two definitions are in the *Treatise* given as "presenting a different view of the same object, and making us consider it either as a *philosophical* or as a *natural* relation . . ." (I (iii) 14, p. 170). Relations of the former sort relate things or objects under investigation, relations of the latter kind relate ideas in the minds of investigators. The labels are confusing, and the situation is not much helped if we try to associate philosophical relations with natural philosophy and natural relations with human nature.

In so far as our interests are philosophical, Hume's accounts of causation as a natural relation have little to offer us. For, when anyone asserts that this is a or the cause of that, they are certainly not saying anything about either their own associations of ideas or their lack of such associations. At most such stories could perhaps suggest how it is that we come to cherish whatever misconceptions about objective causal necessities we had previously been shown to harbour. We should remember too that, on Hume's principles, to track down the impression from which the idea of causally necessary connection is derived must be to legitimate that idea. Nevertheless, and very understandably, he himself at times appears inclined to see his supposed discoveries here as providing: not so much a legitimation, and perhaps clarification, of a fundamental and indispensable notion; but rather the revelatory detection of the true source of a popular misconception.

In the *Treatise* causation as a philosophical relation is defined as involving "An object precedent and contiguous to another, and where all the objects resembling the former are plac'd in like relations of precedency and contiguity to those objects that resemble the latter" (I (iii) 14, p. 170). But when later he came "to cast . . . that work anew" there was a very significant addition, but made without explanation or justification. We now have, much as before, "*an object, followed by another, and where all the objects similar to the first are followed by objects similar to the second*". But here a second sentence follows: "Or in other words *where, if the first object had not been, the second never had existed*" (EHU VII (ii), p. 76).

As on one previous occasion the clause following "Or in other words" is neither equivalent to nor deducible from the clause preceding. And, once again, this unnoticed non-equivalence is of crucial importance. Certainly the first clause does faithfully epitomize Hume's account of causation as a philosophical relation: all that there is out there in the External World – and, for that matter, in the minds studied by those whom Hartley was later to christen psychologists – is constant conjunction and regular succession. This relation can be sufficiently symbolized as a material implication – not as a matter of fact A and not B: i.e., for those sold on symbolism, $\sim(A. \sim B)$. If this were indeed all that there was to it, then it would no longer be self-contradictory and irrecoverably absurd to talk of backwards causation.

But, as we shall see, there is much more to it; while it has been precisely their uncritical acceptance of a pure regularity or material implication account of causation which has misled some otherwise well-girded philosophers to give hospitality to that nonsensical suggestion (Flew, 1954; and contrast Ayer, 1956, pp. 192-8). The crux is this. Whereas the first clause of this revised 'definition' does faithfully epitomize Hume's account of causation as a philosophical relation, the second expresses a proposition of a kind which no such account can entail, yet which every causal and indeed every nomological proposition must entail. Hume's throwaway addition is, therefore, something which no Humian account can embrace, yet something for which any alternative which is to be adequate must make provision.

For that second clause expresses a subjunctive, contrary-to-fact conditional: "*if the first object had not been, the second never had existed.*" But this conclusion obviously cannot be deduced from any non-nomological generalization stating only, as a matter of unexplained brute fact, that all objects of the first kind always have been, are and will be followed by objects of the second kind. All causal and indeed all nomological propositions, on the other hand, must sustain such inferences. If, for instance, you maintain that the cause of the trouble is a lack of fuel in the tank, this entails that – all other things being equal – had there been fuel in the tank then the machine would have operated. While the defining difference between a non-nomological, brute fact generalization and a nomological stating a supposed law of nature precisely is that the one cannot while the other must sustain contrary-to-fact implications.

Hume's official account, therefore, cannot be defended as an explication of what we are actually saying when we assert causal propositions. The further question, whether it is not, nevertheless, an adequate summary of what and all which we have a right to say is best deferred till a little more has been made of the extreme paradoxicality of that official account. Since Hume himself in his discussions 'Of the Idea of necessary Connexion' mentions the Occasionalists and, in particular, Malebranche, the most piquant way of doing this is to apply Hume's findings to the famous illustration of the two ideal clocks. This was, it will be remembered, offered by Arnold Geulincx, and accepted universally, as the perfect exemplification of constant conjunction without causal connection.

In order to provide for temporal succession, and temporal contiguity, let us stipulate that Clock A should be a split second, yet only a split second, fast on Clock B. Spatial contiguity can be provided just as easily by further stipulating that the two clocks are to be touching. So now – remembering that it has been ruled that both clocks are to run with perfect regularity, without interference, and for all eternity – Hume has everything which he could ask for causation as a philosophical relation. It is equally easy to house Humian causation as a natural relation within the same structure. All we need is to introduce an observer who is, like us, a creature of habit. With this example, finally, the 'objects' are, of course, the tellings of a given o'clock by Clock A and the tellings of the same o'clock by Clock B.

Now, how is it that we can know that the ones are not in fact causing the occurrence of the others? The answer is that we can know this because in our own personal experience, and in the experience of reliable informants, it has been found: that, if you stop or destroy one such clock without touching the other, then that other will continue unaffected; and that, if you try to affect one by manipulating the other, then you will not and cannot succeed.

The grounds of such beliefs, such knowledge, do not lie in any series of impressions impinging upon some inert, solitary, incorporeal Cartesian soul; however uniform these series may have in the past been, or however uniform we may complacently expect them for the future to remain. It is, Hume has surely shown, impossible to derive the ideas of causal necessity or causal connection from the idea of merely observed constant conjunction! Instead the grounds of such beliefs, of such knowledge, lie in our experience of activity, as creatures of flesh and blood operating in a mind-independent world: experience of trying to push or to pull things about, and of succeeding in pushing or pulling some but not others; experience of wondering what would happen if, of experimenting, and thus of discovering through experiment what in truth does happen when; and so on, and on and on. To our knowledge of causal, and indeed of all other nomological propositions, we may apply the last words of an epitaph for one of Stalin's many murdered henchpersons, S. M. Kirov: "Only in constant action was his constant certainty found" (Sloan, 1938, p. 179).

It is thus that as agents we acquire the idea of causation, and its component notions of practical (as opposed to logical) necessity and of practical (as opposed to logical) impossibility. 'Component' is the word, since causing is making something happen; and since, in this sense of the word 'cause', making something happen is bringing it about that its happening is practically necessary while its not happening is practically impossible (Black, 1958).

It is, we may remark parenthetically, precisely because causing is thus making things happen – because the relation of effects to causes is not merely one of regular succession – that talk of backwards causation is so egregiously absurd. It is absurd, however seemingly sophisticated the talkers. For such causation would have to involve: either making something to have happened, which had in fact already happened without benefit of any later 'making'; or else making something to have happened or not to have happened although that something had already not happened or, as the case might be, happened. To attempt the former would be sufficiently redundant and ridiculous. But to attempt the latter must raise the most pressing questions about the attemptor's sanity.

Returning to the mainstream, it is from the two complementary notions of practical necessity and practical impossibility – a pair essential to both causes (in this sense) and to laws of nature – that subjunctive, contrary-to-fact conclusions follow. If we know only that, as a matter of unexplained brute fact, all As have been, are and will be succeeded by Bs, then we are in no position to draw any deductions about might have beens. But when we know that it is practically necessary for As to be followed by Bs and practically impossible for such successions not to occur, then we can confidently and correctly infer that if there were to have been an A in some place and at some time, where and when there was in fact no A, then it would have been succeeded by a B.

It is important, finally, to emphasize again that and how Hume's position here is, as so often elsewhere, conditioned by his three Cartesian presuppositions. For if all our knowledge is, as Hume would wish, to be founded on experience, and if – the Big If – we have to construe the word 'experience' in that blinkered and artificial manner; then there is indeed no way in which we can either acquire concepts containing a contrary-to-fact element or justify assertions involving such concepts. Allow that observers who were not and never had been agents might conceivably become aware: not only of some singular facts; but also of the subsistence of certain constant conjunctions between occurrences of different sorts. Still it has surely by now become beyond dispute that observers so pure, so inert, and so congenitally impotent, could not have acquired the concept of causing, of making something happen. Much less then could they be or become in a position to cite experiential reason for holding that this is indeed causing that. Nor is it only the concept of cause, it is too every other notion containing the idea of the contrary-to-fact, which is and has to be both derived from, and justified by reference to, our fundamental and universal human experience of agency, and of having the ability to act or not to act, at will.

Credit, at last, where credit is due; and much too rarely given. Berkeley, and others, are often, quite rightly, reproached for insisting that it is agents alone which can be causes. (Berkeley, of course, also believed that agents are all and only incorporeal spiritual substances: see, for instance, *Principles*, §§ 105-8, or the Letter to Johnson dated 25/XI/29, § 2.) But Berkeley and these others are not, as they should be, credited with the genuine insight that human agency is and must be our paradigm case; albeit a paradigm which permits extension to cover all manner of causes which are not agents. It must be. For how could your perfectly pure observer, an inert, incorporeal subject of exclusively private experience, a creature necessarily incapable of any action either physical or mental – how could such a wretch acquire the concept of agency?

Although Hume's official view is always that causation as a philosophical relation is nothing but regular succession, he does in both his treatments let slip references suggesting something other or more. We have already given a lot of attention to one of these, the casual addition to the 'definition' in the first *Enquiry*. But there are other, more direct hints of the crucial importance of agency, although Hume makes nothing of them. For instance, at one point in the *Treatise* Hume writes: "We have no other notion of cause and effect, but that of certain objects, which have been *always conjoin'd* together, and which in all past instances have been found inseparable" (I (iii) 6, p. 93). How, he ought to have asked himself, has this been found if not through repeated but always unsuccessful efforts to disrupt the correlation?

Here, as in his account of the origins of our beliefs about the External World, Hume sometimes forgets his Cartesian presuppositions; though the offences are certainly more flagrant and more frequent there. He must not, however, be reproached harshly. For all those, and they have been many, who have accepted those wildly unrealistic yet vastly seductive presuppositions have always found it practically impossible to maintain them consistently. Berkeley, for instance, in the *Principles*, tries to be a phenomenalist about his study table, but nevertheless continues brazenly to assume, what he elsewhere so famously and so brilliantly denies, that there is a mind-independent world, with objects occupying and moving between positions in that world: "The table I write on I say exists; that is, I see and feel it: and if I were out of my study I should say it existed; meaning thereby that if I was in my study I might perceive it, or that some other spirit does perceive it" (I 3, p. 259: and compare Cowley, 1968, passim).


## 2 EVIDENCING THE OCCURRENCE OF MIRACLES

Hume's discussion 'Of Miracles' was, beyond doubt, the most provocative publication of his lifetime. It was primarily, as he was complacently to notice in the Autobiography, to this that "Answers by Reverends and Right Reverends come out two or three in a year . . ." Once when "in good company", Hume complained that he was condemned for so small a proportion of his total output, "an honest fellow" delighted him with a memorably apt comment: "Damn'd cutting indeed, but excellent." That "honest fellow" had recalled "an Acquaintance of mine, a Notary public, who having been condemn'd to be hang'd for Forgery, lamented the Hardship of his Case, that after having written many Thousand inoffensive Sheets, He shou'd be hang'd for one line" (Mossner, 1954, p. 545).

Two points must be stated and stressed from the start. The first is that Hume was engaged with a question of evidence rather than a question of fact. What he was trying to establish was: not that miracles do not occur, although he does make it very plain that this was his own view as well as that of all other men of sense; but that, whether or not they did or had, this is not something we can any of us ever be in a position positively to know. This is why the label 'Hume's Check' fits, whereas 'Hume's Checkmate' would not.

The second is that the argument of this Section X is relevant to much more than some admittedly crucial questions of religious belief. Certainly Hume's prime concern within the context of the first *Enquiry* is to interdict the development of the second stage of the standard rational apologetic for Christianity; showing "that a miracle can never be proved, so as to be the foundation of a system of religion" (X (ii), p. 127). But, both in this section and elsewhere, Hume makes it very clear that he is interested in, and wishes to promote, a much more general application of his argument. So it is a noteworthy index of the blinkering power of academic compartmentalization that, in *The Presuppositions of Critical History*, F. H. Bradley should have made no mention of Hume as a predecessor; while, in *The Idea of History*, R. G. Collingwood saw Hume's methodological contribution as confined to the *Treatise* and to the *History* itself. The unexamined and manifestly mistaken assumption here appears to be that, if something is a contribution to the philosophy of religion, then it cannot at one and the same time be a contribution to the philosophy of the social sciences, or of anything else.

(i) After a mischievous reference to an intellectual indiscretion of the Latitudinarian theologian and future Archbishop Tillotson, Hume announces that he has "discovered an argument of like nature, which if just, will with the wise and learned, be an everlasting check to all kinds of superstitious delusion, and consequently, will be useful as long as the world endures. For so long, I presume, will the accounts of miracles and prodigies be found in all history, sacred and profane"

(X (i), p. 110). Hume's Check is thus presented as an essentially defensive argument, which promises to enable "A wise man", who "proportions his belief to the evidence", to dismiss the "impertinent solicitations" of every kind of "bigotry and superstition" (ibid., p. 110).

The heart of the matter is that, "from the nature of the fact", there must always be a conflict in the evidence required to establish the occurrence of a miracle. "A miracle", Hume explains, "may be accurately defined, *a transgression of a law of nature by a particular volition of the Deity, or by the interposition of some invisible agent*" (ibid., p. 115).

Critics have, of course, laboured to fault this "accurate definition". But to all such objections there are two together decisive replies. In the first place, it is in fact substantially the same as that employed by the most distinguished writer among Hume's contemporary opponents: "a work effected in a manner . . . different from the common and regular method of providence, by the interposition either of God himself, or of some intelligent agent superior to man, for the proof or evidence of some particular doctrine, or in attestation of the authority of some particular person" (Clarke, 1738, II, p. 701). Second, and still more to the point, miracles have to be conceived in this kind of way, if their occurrence is, as desired, to serve as a Divine endorsement of some "system of religion". For only some such overriding of a strong order of Nature could be sufficient to require us to postulate an intervention by the hand of God.

But now, clearly, the evidence for the subsistence of such a strong order of Nature will have to be put on the side of the balance opposite to that containing the evidence for the occurrence of the exceptional overriding. (Hume even at this stage still likes to think of weighings of evidence in rather crudely mechanical and quantitative terms.) " 'The plain consequence is," he concludes at the end of Part I of Section X, "That no testimony is sufficient to establish a miracle, unless the testimony be of such a kind, that its falsehood would be more miraculous, than the fact, which it endeavours to establish; and even in that case there is a mutual destruction of arguments, and the superior only gives us an assurance suitable to that degree of force, which remains, after deducting the inferior' " (p. 116).

(ii) In Part II Hume becomes more particular, insisting – contrary to his previous "too liberal . . . concession" – "that there never was a miraculous event established on so full an evidence" (p. 116).

Here we find many sound but strictly non-philosophical points. Anyone who has had practical experience of investigation into such matters must resonate to some of Hume's observations, both on the psychology of testimony and on the remoteness in both space and time of what seem at first sight to be the strongest cases. We should do well also to take to heart Hume's advice to suspect "every relation . . . which depends in any degree upon religion" (p. 129), and to extend it to include all material which is, in the broadest sense, ideologically sensitive.

Most of the Founding Fathers of parapsychology, for instance, who came together in 1882 to establish the Society of Psychical Research, hoped that its investigations might – by falsifying monistic, Aristotelian views of the nature of man, and by supporting what we have distinguished as the third of Hume's Cartesian presuppositions – provide support for some less materialist and more spiritual world-outlook than those which they saw as encouraged by developments in the mainstream sciences. One of Hume's most distinguished contemporaries expressed that same hope very forcefully: "If but one account of the intercourse of men with separate spirits be admitted, their whole castle in the air (Deism, atheism, materialism) falls to the ground" (Wesley, 1827, V, p. 265).

All this is perhaps all very well; or, rather, it would be if Section X was not subsequent to Sections V and VII. For in those earlier sections Hume has disqualified himself from appealing to the subsistence of laws of nature, at least in any understanding which would make an overriding of such laws require an exercise of Supernatural power. He is, therefore, entitled to employ his check only as an argumentum ad hominem. This would certainly not devalue it as a purely defensive intellectual tactic; notwithstanding that the implications for Hume as a positive moral scientist must be catastrophic. For any opponent wanting to make much of alleged overridings becomes thereby and necessarily committed to maintaining that there are known and strong laws, the overriding of which must be sufficiently remarkable to warrant an intellectual revolution.

In fact, Hume writes as if he had never for a moment doubted the known reality of practical necessity and practical impossibility – except when he is directly discussing and in effect denying both! He does not scruple to assert that "In such conclusions as are founded on an infallible experience . . . A wise man . . . expects the event with the last degree of assurance, and regards his past experience as a full *proof* of the future existence of that event" (X (i), p. 110).

Again, Hume seems not a whit embarrassed to maintain that there is a great gulf between the merely marvellous and the truly miraculous, although he himself has made and can make no provision for any such distinction: "But in order to encrease the probability against the testimony of witnesses, let us suppose that the fact, which they affirm, instead of being only marvellous, is really miraculous . . . A miracle is a violation of the laws of nature; and as a firm and unalterable experience has established these laws, the proof against a miracle, from the very nature of the fact, is as entire as any argument from experience can possibly be imagined" (ibid., p. 114). In the *History* too Hume preserves the same confident composure. Thus, in treating the story of Joan of Arc, he insists: "It is the business of history to distinguish between the *miraculous* and the *marvellous*: to reject the first in all narrations merely profane and human; to doubt the second; and when obliged by unquestionable testimony . . . to receive as little as is consistent with the known facts and circumstances" (Hume, 1754-62, II, p. 398).

(iii) But let us cease from cavilling; and, taking up again the hints provided by the references here to "an infallible experience" and to "a firm and unalterable experience", let us try to learn whatever lessons there are to be learnt about the presuppositions and the methods which are essential to critical history – and equally essential, perhaps, to the investigation of the putative prodigies of parapsychology. The place to start is the *Treatise*, at the one relevant passage, noticed by Collingwood: ". . . when we see certain characters or figures describ'd upon paper, we infer that the person, who produc'd them, would affirm such facts, the death of *Caesar*, the success of *Augustus*, the cruelty of *Nero* . . ." (I (iii) 1, pp. 404-5).

Now compare this with the Additional Note about those miracles "which were lately said to have been wrought in France upon the tomb of Abbé Paris, the famous Jansenist." This case was doubly interesting to Hume: both because he had himself been in France at the time; and because both the Jansenists and their rivals the Jesuits were fully agreed that miracles occurring under the auspices of either party would constitute a decisive endorsement of the doctrines of that party, and an equally decisive discrediting of the doctrines of their opponents. Hume emphasizes that the very able investigating magistrate in Paris was wholeheartedly committed to exploding the claims of the Jansenists: "In the case of Mademoiselle Thibaut he sent the famous De Sylva to examine her; whose evidence is very curious. The physician declares, that it was impossible that she could have been so ill as was proved by witnesses; because it was impossible that she could, in so short a time, have recovered so perfectly as he found her. He reasoned, like a man of sense, from natural causes . . ." (EHU X (ii), pp. 124 and 345).

Taken together these two passages show, what Hume never manages outright to say, that the critical historian, in approaching the detritus of the past, has to assume whatever he knows, or thinks that he knows, about what is probable or improbable, possible or impossible. For it is only upon these always fallible and always corrigible assumptions that he becomes able to interpret any of that detritus as historical evidence at all; much less to erect upon it his account of what did and did not actually happen. Thus, in the *Treatise* passage, we see the historian arguing that, since ink marks of this kind can be produced on old pieces of paper only by human writing, we have here some items of documentary evidence. Then, in the passage from the first *Enquiry*, we have a physician doing a bit of historical work; arguing that the testimonial evidence in the case of Mademoiselle Thibaut has got to be mistaken, since what was said to have happened was downright impossible.

Where Hume himself went seriously wrong, lapsing from his own high corrigibilist principles, was in taking it for granted that everything which an eighteenth-century man of sense believed to be impossible must in truth actually be impossible. He was thus misled to reject the accounts of supposed miracles said to have been wrought in Egypt by the Roman soldier Emperor Vespasian. But a re-examination, in the light of the later progress of psychosomatic medicine, of the evidence provided by Suetonius and Tacitus strongly suggests that the events reported did occur; but if so, of course, were not miraculous (Flew, 1961, pp. 183-4 and 194ff.).

The fact that Hume seems to have fallen into substantive error as a result of accepting those presuppositions, and following those methods, which we have contended to be essential to critical history, must not be construed as showing that such presuppositions or such methods are either irrational or in some other way misguided. For there is no alternative and better way open to anyone who wishes to discover what actually happened. Indeed it is only and precisely by accepting similar presuppositions, and by following similar methods, that later workers have become able to correct Hume's substantive mistakes.

Where Hume did go wrong, and where he fell sadly from his own highest state of grace, was in failing to recognize, and to allow for, the possibility, and the likelihood, that some of the particular beliefs which he and his contemporaries cherished about what is or is not probable or possible would later turn out to have been in error. For, so long as the sciences continue to progress, historians will be by their cloth required from time to time to review that progress; asking themselves whether further historical evidence might not now be extracted from the still surviving detritus of the past, and which previous conclusions based upon since exploded misconceptions now need to be revised or rejected.

Two examples of developments which have made possible the extraction of historical evidence from formerly silent materials are radio-carbon dating and dating by comparing the intervals between the annual growth lines in timber. Both of these developments occurred long after Hume's time. But an ideal example of what had been a reasonable conclusion based upon a belief which was later decisively discredited could have been employed by Hume, although it appears in fact to have been first introduced into this discussion a century later by F. H. Bradley. In Herodotus, 'the Father of Critical History', we read that at the time of the Pharaoh Necho II (about 600 BC) Phoenician sailors claimed to have circumnavigated Africa. They said that they had sailed South down what we call the Red Sea and arrived at the Mediterranean coast of Egypt nearly three years later. The interesting thing for us is their report that during the voyage the position of the Sun shifted from the South to the North, and back again. Herodotus, recording that they said this, states that he himself does not believe what they said. He had two good reasons for disbelief: first, he knew that Phoenician and other sailors were apt to tell tall tales; and second, he took it that he knew that what the sailors reported was impossible. Herodotus therefore had good reason to dismiss this story; and in fact, following the soundest principles of critical method, he did dismiss it.

Yet what was for Herodotus an excellent reason for incredulity is for us –and could have been for Hume had he happened to notice this example – the decisive ground for believing that Phoenicians did in fact circumnavigate Africa at this time. They could scarcely have got this thing about the changing relative position of the Sun right unless they had actually made the voyage which they said they had made. Both Herodotus and the successors who have on this point corrected him were employing the same sound historical methods, the only methods possible for the critical historian.

Both he and we, that is, are and cannot but be committed, in interpreting and assessing the detritus of the past as historical evidence, to appealing to all that we know or think we know about what is probable or improbable, possible or impossible. Thus Herodotus, in trying to interpret the evidence of the Phoenicians, rightly appealed to what he knew, or thought he knew, about astronomy and geography. We, following exactly the same fundamental principles of historical reconstruction, but having the advantage over him of knowing more about astronomy and geography, reach different conclusions, albeit by fundamentally the same methods.

(iv) One further, final finding remains to be considered. It concerns the reactions of the "man of sense", reasoning "from natural causes", to the possibility that – notwithstanding everything so far said to the contrary – there may "be miracles, or violations of the usual course of nature, of such a kind as to admit of proof from human testimony; though, perhaps, it will be impossible to find any such in all the records of history" (EHU X (ii), p. 127). This modest and qualified concession comes immediately after the insistence that what has been established is, simply yet sufficiently, "that a miracle can never be proved, so as to be the foundation of a system of religion." Notice too that here, in spelling out the meaning of the term 'miracle', Hume quietly replaces his former "violations of the laws of nature" by the far weaker expression "violations of the usual course of nature".

Hume proceeds next to deploy two imaginary cases. First, "suppose all authors, in all languages, agree, that, from the first of January 1600, there was a total darkness over the whole earth for eight days . . ." (p. 127). Second, "suppose that all . . . who treat of England, should agree that, on the first of January 1600, Queen Elizabeth died; . . . and that, after being interred a month, she again appeared, resumed the throne, and governed England for three years" (p. 128).

To no one's surprise, and although the evidence for this Elizabethan fantasy has been supposed immeasurably stronger than that available in the actual case of the alleged Resurrection of Jesus bar Joseph, Hume does not hesitate for a moment before putting that second supposition down as forever unbelievable. Then, as if the intended moral was not already sufficiently sharp, he adds a fiercely pointed paragraph on how the story would become even more incredible if "this miracle" were "ascribed to any new system of religion" (p. 128). To the first supposition, on the other hand, there are at least some analogies in our experience. So "it is evident that our present philosophers, instead of doubting the fact, ought to receive it as certain, and ought to search for the causes whence it might be derived" (p. 128).

Since "our present philosophers" are certainly our scientists, and since the causes sought are presumably natural causes, Hume's concession turns out to be nothing of the sort. Indeed, given that Hume is working with a definition which stipulates that the occurrence of a miracle requires some Supernatural intervention, the suggestion that such an occurrence might be proved, provided only that it gave no support to "a system of religion", becomes doubtfully coherent. The most charitable construction to be put on these few remarks is that he is saying, or at any rate suggesting, something about the relations between history on the one hand and the natural sciences on the other; an interpretation which makes Collingwood's inability to grasp the secular relevance of this section all the more regrettable.

To appreciate what is at stake we need perhaps a more persuasive supposition. So suppose that European astronomers, when word first reached them of the eclipse observations made centuries earlier in China, had been committed to a theory precluding the occurrence of any eclipses visible at any of the times or in any of the places listed in the Chinese records. Then, if there was no independent reason for suspecting the truth of those Chinese observations – no state ideology, for instance, to be supported by the occurrence of eclipses in those places and at those times – it would surely have been right for the European astronomers to have had urgent second thoughts about the truth of the theory, and the supposed laws, from which they had inferred the impossibility of the occurrence of such eclipses.

As Hume might better have put it, our past philosophers, instead of (not doubting but) denying the alleged facts, ought (if not to have received them as certain then at least) to have allowed them to be possible, and ought to have searched for the causes from which they might have been derived; (causes which would show such occurrences to have been not practically impossible but practically necessary). In the meantime our past historians, instead of flatly repudiating the claims in the Chinese records, should presumably have returned the peculiarly Scottish verdict of 'Not proven'.

Everything here depends upon the differences in logical strength between typical propositions in history and in the natural sciences, and upon the corresponding differences in the strength of the best evidence which we can have for the truth of propositions of these two disparate kinds. Since Hume's explicit account of causation, as well as the account of laws of nature implicit therein, can find no room either for practical necessities and practical impossibilities, or for the contrary-to-fact truths deducible therefrom, he becomes quite unable either to explain these differences or to justify the methodological consequences following from them. Yet once these deficiencies have been made good everything falls into place.

The historical propositions, in this case the propositions stating that an eclipse was visible in such and such a place at such and such a time, are all singular and in the past tense. It is always and necessarily too late now for any direct verification or falsification. If we are ever to discover what actually happened, this can only be by finding something present which can be interpreted as evidence, and by assessing what and how much that available evidence shows.

It is altogether different with nomological propositions; propositions, that is, which state that causal connections or laws of nature obtain; and which necessarily imply something about practical necessity and practical impossibility. Nomological propositions are open and general. They can, at least in principle, be tested for truth or falsity at any time or in any place. Precisely that is why it is reasonable and right for the critical historian to employ all available confirmed nomologicals as canons of exclusion, ruling out many conceivable and even sometimes seemingly well-evidenced occurrences as practically impossible. Yet in doing this our historians should always be aware that steady advances in our knowledge of nomologicals, and occasional upsets revealing that what we had believed to constitute such knowledge was not, may demand historical reassessments – as in the cases of the supposed miracles of Vespasian and the alleged Phoenician circumnavigation of Africa.

(For a much more exhaustive treatment of this Section X, albeit a treatment putting too little emphasis upon Hume's failure to allow for practical necessity and practical impossibility, compare Flew, 1961, chapter VIII.)

# 6

# People: their Minds, their Souls
# or their 'Selves'

Chapter 1 emphasized that Hume's starting point in philosophy was the position which Descartes had reached by the end of the second paragraph of Part IV of the *Discourse*. It also distinguished the three propositions in which that position consisted as Hume's "interlocking Cartesian assumptions". The third of these is most prominent in two sections of Book I of the *Treatise*: 'Of the immateriality of the soul'; and 'Of personal identity'. Although Hume did offer some despairing second thoughts in an appendix to Book III, there is no reconsideration of these topics in the first *Enquiry*. The one further contribution which should be taken into account along with these two sections is the posthumously published essay 'Of the Immortality of the Soul'.

This last material, which is very obviously although never explicitly directed against the immortalist case made by Butler in the *Analogy*, could well have been one of those "nobler parts" which had to be excised in order to fit the *Treatise* to be seen by that good Doctor's eyes. It might have been incorporated into the aggressively agnostic project of *An Enquiry concerning Human Understanding*. For the mortalist conclusions of this essay support the thesis that both our theoretical investigations and our practical concerns should be limited to this world and to this life. However, the first unequivocal references to any such document come in the correspondence about what eventually became the *Four Dissertations* of 1757. Hume's first thought after Lord Stanhope had persuaded him to withdraw the paper on geometry was to substitute two other essays: 'Of the Immortality of the Soul'; and 'Of Suicide'. But other friends persuaded Hume that it would be imprudent to publish either of these at that time. On his deathbed he took pains to ensure that, like the *Dialogues*, these should be published posthumously. They in fact appeared for the first time in the 1777 edition of his *Essays*.

As has been noted already, both at the beginning of chapter 1 and similarly in section 3 of chapter 2, the most remarkable thing about Hume's discussions of personal identity and personal immortality is his uncritical acceptance of the Cartesian conclusion that we persons are all essentially incorporeal: "From that I knew that I was a substance the whole essence or nature of which is to think, and for its existence there is no need of any place, nor does it depend on any material thing; so that this 'me', that is to say, the soul by which I am what I am, is entirely distinct from body, and is even more easy to know than is the latter; and, even if body were not, the soul would not cease to be what it is" (Descartes, 1637, I, p. 101).

Although Hume disagrees with what Descartes goes on to say about the survival and immortality of human souls, the only part of this first conclusion which he is prepared to challenge is the notion that what Descartes is supposed to mean by 'thoughts' must inhere in, or be otherwise essentially related to, some spiritual substance; whatever that might be. (Rather than 'thoughts' Hume himself prefers to speak either of ideas and impressions or of perceptions of the mind.) To the Cartesian spiritual substance Hume's own self-consciously radical alternative is to urge that, as people, we are: not the allegedly mysterious and elusive substances which are the subjects or the havens of Cartesian thoughts; but nothing else but mere collections of such entities, supposedly occurring independently. He contends that it is not substantial 'selves' or minds or souls but these which are what the Scholastics would have described as the subsistent things, substances of which we can coherently speak as existing separately – existing, that is, independent of anyone or of any thing which might significantly be said to have or to suffer or in some other way to be characterized by such affections of consciousness.

Both the original Cartesian conclusion, which Hume accepts, and the counter-contention, which he presses as in effect an amendment, are irredeemably erroneous; and both go wrong for the same reason. In the first place, both the word 'person' itself and all the other person-words – such as the personal pronouns and terms like 'butcher' or 'politician', picking out members of classes of functionary – are themselves words for members of a kind – our own kind – of creatures of flesh and blood. If anyone doubts this, let them ask how they learnt the meanings of such words, and how they would teach those meanings either to their own children or to other people.

It is, therefore, clear that people cannot be simply and straightforwardly identified with their 'selves' or their minds or their souls. This given, it then becomes obvious that no person's soul or mind or 'self' can itself be picked out and fixed as a determinate subject of discourse without reference to, and independent of, the particular person whose soul or mind or 'self' it is. It is all too easy, yet it is altogether wrong, to slip inattentively and without warrant from a familiar truth to a fantastic falsehood: to start by being aware that everyone can understand the statements that Janet has a soul above sex, or that Jack has a criminal mentality; but to conclude that sense has been given to talk of Janet's soul and of Jack's mind surviving the deaths and dissolutions of the both of them, and so proceeding to their equally just (and therefore necessarily unequal) individual rewards (Flew, 1964, Introduction and passim; and compare Flew, 1981, ch. II).

To put the crucial point in another way, the mistake is to interpret the words 'mind' and 'soul' as words referring to a sort of substance, something which could sensibly be said to survive the death and dissolution of the flesh-and-blood person whose mind or soul it is – or was. The truth is that all those well understood weekday utterances employing the word 'mind' constitute slightly more picturesque but rather less precise ways of saying things about the abilities, affections, dispositions and other characteristics of those familiar objects of often too, too solid flesh – persons (Ryle, 1949).

The plain yet to many most unwelcome consequence is that, if there is to be a survival hypothesis which is not already known to be false, then those proposing to put this bold conjecture forward must needs introduce first a new concept of incorporeal person: showing too that and how an individual belonging to this supposedly possible new species could, after all, be one and the same with one of the old familiar, essentially material kind. This would certainly be no easy task. Indeed – to put it mildly – it is doubtful whether it could be achieved. For how could any such essentially incorporeal being be identified; or, if ever once identified, reidentified through time? And then, even if that could be done, how could any such outré entity be shown to be really the same as some workaday creature of flesh and blood (Flew, 1976a, chs. 8-11)?

The mistake in the original Cartesian conclusion consists, therefore, in first equating people with their souls or minds or 'selves', and then misconstruing the words 'souls' or 'minds' or 'selves' as words for a sort or sorts of substances. The mistake in Hume's counter-contention is of the same kind. For he insists on asserting that "perceptions of the mind" can be said to be either "loose and separate" or arranged in an as it were "bundle or collection". But the truth is that always and necessarily such moments of consciousness come – shall we say? – prepackaged. It is altogether absurd and preposterous: first to try to refer to one particular idea or impression as being – for all you know – unowned and unhad; and then to attempt to discover whose particular idea or impression it either is, or was, or will be.

Remarkable though it is, both that Hume should have accepted that particular Cartesian conclusion so uncritically, and that he should have urged his own amending contention so confidently, it is perhaps still more remarkable that so few of his critics appear to have jibbed persistently. Many philosophers have themselves accepted all the three contentions previously distinguished as constituting the extreme sceptical position of Descartes, although like Hume they have usually been most explicit in their emphasis upon the second. This is true, for instance, of the entire logical empiricist tradition from Karl Pearson and Ernst Mach before the First World War, on through the Vienna Circle of Logical Positivists between the wars, and after (Ayer, 1946; and compare Flew, 1978a, ch. 10). It is true also of one who was in its day the leading local dissident from that circle. Already in section 2 of chapter 4 we saw that Sir Karl Popper seems still to accept one if not both the first two of these three Cartesian contentions. Even more remarkably, *The Self and Its Brain* shows absolutely no awareness of the difficulties afflicting the confidently reiterated third – that there is a substantial yet incorporeal subject of consciousness (Popper and Eccles, 1977, ch. P 4 and passim).

Other philosophers, while themselves dissenting more or less extensively from this tradition, have nevertheless neglected to stress, from the beginning, that and how Hume's whole approach to the problems of the present chapter is fundamentally wrong-headed. Thus the author of one of the best general books about Hume, an author who had himself previously published two most useful papers in this particular area, entitles the relevant chapter of that book 'The Self'

(Penelhum, 1975). If only he had recognized that that expression is a philosophical technicality, then he would have realized also that the layperson needs to have it explained (Flew, 1950). In providing such an explanation he could scarcely have failed to bring out, sharp and clear, right from the start: both the perversity of construing 'person' as a synonym for 'mind' or 'soul' or 'self'; and the impossibility of identifying either minds, or perceptions of the mind, save by reference to the flesh and blood persons whose minds they are, or of which they must be the 'perceptions'.

### 1 SUBSTANCE OR NOT SUBSTANCE, MATERIAL OR IMMATERIAL?

Some forty pages before he begins to address himself to the problem, Hume, equating "these ideas of self and person", gives notice that, on this assumption, "there is no question in philosophy more abstruse than that concerning identity, and the nature of the uniting principle, which constitutes a person." This observation is made in the course of inquiring "how far we are *ourselves* the objects of our senses". The question is alleged to be difficult, presumably because Hume believes that "in common life 'tis evident these ideas of self and person are never very fix'd nor determinate." He concludes: "'Tis absurd, therefore, to imagine the senses can ever distinguish between ourselves and external objects" (THN I (iv) 2, pp. 189–90).

It is an index of the extent to which Hume's Cartesian assumptions have been shared that so few critics appear to have recognized that it is, rather, his own abrupt and negative conclusion which is the absurdity. For a start, it is only philosophers and perhaps psychologists who ever speak of selves or The Self; although everybody, specialists and laypersons both, employs, and possesses a sufficiently clear understanding of, the reflexive personal pronouns – 'himself', 'herself', 'myself', 'yourself', and so on (Flew, 1950). In that everyday understanding there can be no question but that we can be "*ourselves* the objects of our senses" to exactly the same extent as to each of us "external objects" are also "objects of our senses". To each of us individually, both ourselves – whether directly or with mirrors – and everyone else and every other non-human thing are equally "objects"; and, in an understanding in which we ourselves are what other "objects" are external to, they are also "external objects". For a provident Nature has supplied us all with the skins by which every individual person is, in a very fixed and determinate fashion, separated and distinguished from all the rest of the furniture of the Universe. Since they have almost always been overlooked, these excruciatingly elementary objections do need to be laboured now.

(i) The section 'Of personal identity' is immediately preceded by another, 'Of the immateriality of the soul'. Here Hume's first challenge "to certain philosophers", unnamed, concerns "the material or immaterial substances, in which they suppose our perceptions to inhere" (THN I (iv) 5, p. 232). It would, he urges, be an evasion to reply "that the definition of a substance is *something which may exist by itself*; and that this definition ought to satisfy us" (p. 233). Whether or not it ought to serve as the sufficient last word, this definition certainly is directed at the relevant sense of the term 'substance'.

Hume responds by maintaining "that this definition agrees to every thing that can possibly be conceiv'd." Appealing to some of his own distinctive fundamental principles, he concludes, "that since all our perceptions are different from each other, and from every thing else in the universe, they are also distinct and separable, and may be consider'd as separately existent, and may exist separately, and have no need of any thing else to support their existence. They are, therefore, substances as far as this definition explains a substance" (p. 233).

If indeed it does follow from those distinctively Humian fundamental principles that sense-data can significantly be said to exist unsensed by anybody, or that a throbbing pain could intelligibly be asserted to occur loose and separate, and not as the pain suffered by a particular person, then that constitutes a sufficient reason first to rethink and then at least in part to reject those principles. Hume, however, in the earlier section 'Of abstract ideas', has volunteered "to explain that *distinction of reason*, which is so much talk'd of, and is so little understood, in the schools" (THN I (i) 7, p. 24). Whether or not we are prepared to admit that explanation, Hume's own admission of such distinctions of reason itself concedes that sometimes what we can separately conceive could not be conceived as existing separately. We can for instance, perfectly well discuss a shape without mentioning either a size or any object so shaped. We can also review sorts of sense-data without stating either that these must be had, or who has them. Yet from none of this can we validly deduce the false conclusion that both shapes and sense-data are, in the appropriate sense, substances.

(ii) Hume next proceeds to draw as a corollary the further conclusion that we ought not to ask the allegedly meaningless question, "*Whether perceptions inhere in a material or immaterial substance . . .?*" (THN I (iv) 5, p. 234). Since Humian perceptions are moments of consciousness, which any Cartesian must rate as mental (and therefore presumably immaterial), Hume's actual position here comes close to what in Berkeley everyone is content to call immaterialism. Hume himself goes on to take issue with the Cartesian claim that "Thought" (or consciousness) "and extension are qualities wholly incompatible, and never can incorporate together in one subject" (p. 234).

Arguing that, since "the very idea of extension is copy'd from nothing but an impression" (p. 239), both ideas and impressions may be described as extended, Hume sees "The free-thinker turning the tables on his antagonists . . . the . . . Theologians . . ." He does this by challenging them to explain how they think that "they can incorporate a simple and indivisible subject" – the soul as an immaterial spiritual substance – "with an extended perception" (p. 240). While deploying the forces needed to effect this agreeably mischievous and paradoxical confutation Hume takes time off: both to propound the maxim "*that an object may exist, and yet be no where*" (p. 235); and to reiterate what he always takes to be an incontestable truism, "The most vulgar philosophy informs us, that no external object can make itself known to the mind immediately, and without the interposition of an image or perception" (p. 239). In insisting, in a curiously Rylean way, that "A moral reflection cannot be plac'd on the right or on the left hand of a passion . . ." (p. 236), Hume does not draw the explicit moral that, when such positionless entities are either causes or effects, then cause and effect cannot be spatially contiguous. Nevertheless this *Treatise* demand is quietly dropped in the first *Enquiry*.

(iii) "This", Hume continues, "gives me an occasion to take a-new into consideration the question concerning the substance of the soul . . ." He seizes on it as offering an opportunity to indulge himself in a little naughty philosophical fun, maintaining "that the doctrine of the immateriality, simplicity and indivisibility of a thinking substance" lies wide open to all the same objections as the system "for which Spinoza is so universally infamous" (p. 240). This indulgence concluded, Hume proceeds to draw a more particular moral from what previously "has been proved at large . . . that to consider the matter *a priori*, any thing may produce any thing (ibid., p. 247). The particular moral is that there is no force whatever in the Cartesian contention that the ongoings and interactions of merely material bits of stuff could not conceivably either produce or alter any things so totally disparate as states of consciousness.

Certainly Hume has proved his point, which does indeed carry this consequence. Yet the consequence would be much easier to accept if we had not been so strongly assured: both that people are their minds or their souls; and that minds are bundles or collections of momentary states of consciousness. For to most of us this will seem virtually indistinguishable from "the supposition that the soul is immaterial" (Hume, 1741-77, p. 591).

Suppose now that we effect an authentic, and therefore thoroughly unBerkeleyan, return to true common sense. Then at once we realize again what in a way everyone knew before: that persons are a kind of creatures of flesh and blood; that states of consciousness, both human and non-human, are states of paradigmatically material organisms; and that there is, therefore, nothing surprising about the fact that changes in organisms bring about changes in both the non-conscious and the conscious states of these organisms. So it is diametrically wrong to assert that it is a truth, made manifest by the light of nature, "that it is impossible for thought to belong to a material substance." On the contrary: every thought which any of us either has or knows of is, and has to be, a thought of some organism. Yet what is that if it is not "to belong to a material substance"?

(iv) In another digression Hume discusses the implications of endowing the Deity with causal powers: "I answer, that we have no idea of a being endow'd with any power, much less of one endow'd with infinite power" (THN I (iv) 5, p. 248). This discussion has often been overlooked. Selby-Bigge, for instance, in his 'Comparative Tables of the Contents of the *Treatise* and of the *Enquiries*' (pp. xxxiv and xxxv), does not recognize it as an anticipation of sections VII (i) and VIII (ii) of the first. The same discussion could also have supplied useful ammunition for those contending that Hume denied causation. For certainly the denial, in the same paragraph, that there is any "such thing in the universe as a cause or productive principle, not even the deity himself"; does constitute a most categorical denial of efficient causation. But, equally certainly, this is not how Hume himself saw it. If he had, he would not have concluded Part III of Book I with a section 'Rules by which to judge of causes and effects'; a section which anticipates the chapter 'Of the Four Methods of Experimental Inquiry' in Mill's *Logic*.

Finally Hume returns to the official topic of this remarkably rich section. His concluding sentence is the prim and plainly disingenuous statement: "If my philosophy, therefore, makes no addition to the arguments for religion, I have at least the satisfaction to think that it takes nothing from them . . ." (pp. 250-1). Whether or not some draft of his essay 'Of the Immortality of the Soul' was among those "nobler parts" excised in the castration of the *Treatise*, Hume must surely have been aware already that he could and would cut to ribbons both "the moral arguments and those deriv'd from the analogy of nature"; arguments commended in the previous sentence as "equally strong and convincing" (p. 250).


## 2 THE PSYCHOLOGY OF IMMATERIALISM

By adopting the general positions discussed in the previous section Hume becomes in the philosophy of mind committed to answering all particular questions without reference to either the actual or the possible behaviour of the organisms concerned. Some of the awkward consequences of this restriction become apparent right from the beginning. For, when Hume first distinguishes his two categories of "perceptions of the mind", he explains that "The difference betwixt these consists in the degrees of force and liveliness with which they strike upon the mind" (THN I (i) 1, p. 1).

Certainly that difference – one of which the subject must be immediately aware – constitutes a criterion of the kind which his own fundamental principles require him to stipulate. Nevertheless, and equally certainly, it is not of the right kind for his philosophical purposes. What Hume needs – and what, somewhat surreptitiously and elliptically, he forthwith supplies – is intra-mental causes for ideas and extra-mental for impressions. So, on the following page, it appears that there is some other criterion, independent of the "degrees of force and liveliness". For we are told: that, though "The common degrees of these are easily distinguished . . . in particular instances they may very nearly approach to each other"; and that "it sometimes happens that our impressions are so faint and low, that we cannot distinguish them from our ideas."

When, "persuaded of these principles", Hume comes to consider, for instance, memory and imagination, he is bound to insist, as have with less excuse so many later writers, that remembering or imagining must always involve the occurrence of ideas. He is also bound to demand that any one of these sorts of ideas be distinguished from any other: not by the context of behaviour and of dispositions to behave in which its putative members occur; but by some immediately experiencable, peculiar quality in the ideas themselves. These immaterialist inhibitions are most compelling in Book I of the *Treatise*. They begin to weaken in Book II 'Of the Passions', and by Book III have ceased to be noticeably intrusive. On this as on several other counts the sceptical philosopher is, in moving out from his cloistered retirement, transmogrified into the scientific naturalist.

The best case for demonstrating the constricting consequences of such immaterialism in psychology is perhaps provided by Hume's treatment of belief. The *Treatise* formulates the philosophical question, which is our present primary concern: "*Wherein consists the difference betwixt incredulity and belief?*" (I (iii) 7, p. 95). Since Hume at that stage took all thinking to be or involve occurrences of mental imagery, this question presented itself to him as one of distinguishing between two different occurrences of the same thought content; that is to say, presumably the very same set of mental images. His psychological immaterialism then demands that the difference: either be a matter of the occurrence of some extra perception of the mind, along with the having of the relevant set of ideas constituting the thought content; or else be a matter of those constitutive ideas themselves becoming characterized by some immediately experiencable special quality .

What Hume cannot say is that believing is having, or being disposed to have, an extra idea. For this would for him involve that the content of the proposition believed would become different from the content of the same proposition merely supposed or simply entertained. So his first move is to maintain that belief, "as it plainly makes no addition to our precedent ideas, can only change the *manner* of our conceiving them". This change is an increase of "force and vivacity", which makes ideas believed "more strong firm and vivid, than the loose reveries of a castle-builder"(pp. 96 and 97).

In the Appendix, Hume gives his first second thoughts, including a further reason why the crucial differentia cannot be an extra idea: "if belief consisted merely in a new idea, annex'd to the conception, it wou'd be in a man's power to believe what he pleas'd" (p. 624). So the change in "the *manner* of our conceiving" now becomes "a peculiar *feeling* or *sentiment*" which "depends not on the will, but must arise from certain determinate causes and principles . . . of which we are not masters" (pp. 623 and 624). Whereas the increase of "force and vivacity" in the ideas believed might prejudice their claims to re-main ideas rather than impressions, that certain feeling of the Appendix is from the start unequivocally an impression. Hume himself offers no explanation for this change of mind, although the Appendix does withdraw the insistence "that two ideas of the same object can only be different by their different degrees of force and vivacity" (p. 636). Perhaps, in so far as he saw ideas as the stuff of thought and impres-sions as the matter thought about, he was reluctant to find the crucial differentia in that second world.

In the first *Enquiry* the question is posed as one of distinguishing between fiction and belief: "the difference . . . lies in some sentiment or feeling, which is annexed to the latter, not to the former, and which depends not on the will, nor can be commanded at pleasure" (V (ii), p. 48). To provide "a definition of this sentiment" would be "a very difficult, if not an impossible task . . ." So the best thing to be said is that it consists, "not in the peculiar nature or order of ideas, but in the *manner* of their conception and in their *feeling* to the mind." Although "it is impossible perfectly to explain this feeling or manner of concep-tion . . . its true and proper name, as we observed before, is *belief*; which is a term that everyone sufficiently understands in common life" (pp. 48 and 49).

Indeed it is, and indeed we do. Yet Hume cannot be allowed to leave it at that. If his account were correct, then it would be possible to know that Ruth believed the philosophers' familiar but sadly colour-less proposition p only on the basis of her testimony to the occurrence of that essentially private, putative belief-modification or belief-feeling. It is, however, obvious that we are not in fact so constrained.

If we were, we could not follow the wise advice of Descartes – in set-
tling disputed questions about what people sincerely believe to attend
to what they do and do not do, rather than to what they say.

Worse still: if the criterion of belief really were the occurrence of
some peculiar belief-feeling or belief-modification, then – unless that
feeling or that modification were, as apparently it is not, one which
could be adequately identified by some description containing no
reference to belief – it would be in principle impossible to teach the
meaning of the word 'belief'. In that case it could have no meaning,
not at any rate in a public language usable for inter-personal com-
munication. Yet of course it has, and Hume has no doubt of it. Indeed, preposterously, precisely this is his reason for being sure that
everyone will be able to identify that so familiar certain feeling: "But
its true and proper name . . . is *belief*, which term everyone sufficiently understands in common life."

### 3 THE IDENTITY OF BODILESS PERSONS

The upshot of the previous section, therefore, is as negative as it is
decisive. Such fundamental intellectual operations as believing or
remembering or imagining cannot be either distinguished or explained
without reference to the behaviour of organisms; behaviour both verbal and non-verbal, both actual and possible. Certainly a psychology
attending only to behaviour ignores an essential. But more radical,
conceptual impossibilities block the way to any sort of psychology
attending only to consciousness. As we saw in section 3 of chapter 2,
any being which was truly trapped behind a Veil of Ignorance
would be unable to learn whether there were any others caught in the
same predicament. And, as we have just seen, such a being would not
be able to apply these fundamental intellectual concepts to the only
objects of study available to it – the Humian perceptions of its
own mind.

(i) In the present perspective we can see the same section 3 as showing
that this solipsistic cognitive confinement would be even closer than
that. For it must be impossible either to explain what perception is, or
would be, or to distinguish between hallucinatory or otherwise 'wild'
sense-data and the sense-data involved in actual perceiving, without

referring to the mind-independent objects which are perceived, or might be. For the truth is that, properly understood, a Causal Theory of Perception is not, as is so often said, notoriously false. On the contrary: it is necessarily true. What is indeed preposterous and totally discredited is the suggestion that such a lonely prisoner, or some mysteriously coordinated collective of such incurably lonely prisoners, might reasonably hypothesize, and perhaps even come to know, that some of the perceptions of their minds represent, and are caused to occur by, mind-independent objects. It is this "philosophical system" which Hume described as "the monstrous offspring of two principles, which are contrary to each other, which are both at once embrac'd by the mind, and which are unable mutually to destroy each other" (THN I (iv) 2, p. 215).

What is, by contrast, not monstrous but necessary is that the sense-data had by the perceiving subject should be caused to occur by the presence of the object perceived. For suppose that, by suitable stimulation through electrodes in the appropriate areas of their brains, we cause eyeless persons to enjoy the visual sense-data which they would be having if they could see. Then they would, surely, correctly be said at most to 'see' rather than to see; and that even if the objects thus 'seen' were in fact bang in front of their empty eye-sockets?

The outcome of the section 'Of personal identity' is similarly negative, but in this case Hume himself saw it to be so. For in the Appendix he confesses that "upon a more strict review . . . I find myself involv'd in such a labyrinth, that . . . I neither know how to correct my former opinions, nor how to render them consistent" (p. 633). Some modern critics have made heavy weather of his account of his difficulties here. These he sums up by saying that "there are two principles, which I cannot render consistent; nor is it in my power to renounce either of them, viz. *That all our distinct perceptions are distinct existences*, and *that the mind never perceives any real connection among distinct existences*" (p. 636).

For our contemporaries the difficulty is that it is obvious to us, and must surely have been obvious to Hume, that these two principles are perfectly compatible. But consider how theists sometimes present their Problem of Evil. How, they ask, are we to reconcile the goodness of God with his omnipotence? In this case also there is no contradiction between the ideas presented as seemingly irreconcilable. The truly intractable problem is that of squaring this religious hypothesis "with so many undeniable and undenied facts of a manifestly less than perfect Universe". Similarly, for Hume, the problem – the surely equally intractable problem – is to excogitate an answer to the question of personal identity consistent both with the two principles just restated and with his other assumptions?

Already even before Book III and the Appendix had been finally accepted for publication Hume was expressing his disappointment over what appeared to him the generally negative outcome of Book I. This was in a letter to his older friend Francis Hutcheson, a Professor of Philosophy in the University of Glasgow. It was Hutcheson, by the way, who was later to write to Edinburgh urging "that David Hume was not fit for such an office, since among his duties he would have to lecture every Monday on the truth of the Christian religion" (Capaldi, 1975, p. 22). One would like to have heard Hume's response to this objection; while relishing still more the thought of what, had Hume had to deliver them, those Monday lectures might have contained. In that letter to Hutcheson Hume wrote: "I am apt, in a cool hour, to suspect, in general, that most of my Reasonings will be more useful by furnishing Hints and exciting People's Curiosity, than as containing any Principles that will augment the Stock of Knowledge that must pass to future Ages" (Greig, 1932, I, p. 39).

That judgement was far too pessimistic. Certainly, much of Hume's philosophical work, especially in the *Treatise*, has to be scored as negative. Yet it is not on that account nugatory. The crucial transformation required is what in the world of *Smiley's People* is called a turning round. Arguments which had at first appeared to prove outrageous conclusions need to be reversed, being redirected into disproofs of one or more of their own premises. If and when, given Hume's assumptions about the immateriality of the personality and the substantiality of his kind of perception, it seems impossible to develop any consistent and convincing account of the difference between belief and non-belief, and of the nature of either, then it is those assumptions which demand "a more strict review".

Where, on those same assumptions, Hume found a "difficulty . . . too hard for my understanding" (p. 636), there the sympathetic and constructive critic will recognize a major philosophical achievement. For, by showing how impossibly difficult it would be to reidentify through time an individual person conceived as incorporeal, Hume unwittingly demonstrated the correspondingly intractable difficulty of introducing a new concept of incorporeal person; and of supplying effective means both for the identification of such beings, and for their individual reidentification through time. It is, however, this so far unconstructed concept which we have to have if parapsychologists (psychical researchers) are to be able to entertain any survival hypothesis not already known to be false (Flew, 1976a, chs 8–11).

(ii) Hume sets off in fine style: "There are some philosophers, who imagine that we are every moment intimately conscious of what we call our SELF; that we feel its existence and its continuance in existence; and are certain, beyond the evidence of a demonstration, both of its perfect identity and simplicity" (THN I (iv) 6, p. 251). But not, of course, Hume; who, almost if not quite alone, gets things right.

If once we allow that persons are incorporeal, and in view of the fact that none but a rival philosopher would be so prissily affected as to speak of "our SELF" as opposed to ourselves, then we have to concede to Ryle's "ungullible Hume" victory in the first round, on a knockout. For what we may indeed be intimately conscious of when we are aware of ourselves as subjects of experience (in either interpretation of that Janus-faced term), is one particular one of these creatures of flesh and blood which we all in fact are; rather than any incorporeal substance which might or might not be causing us to have some impression from which an idea of self could be derived.

Hume goes on to triumph in successfully not finding that impression: "For my part, when I enter most intimately into what I call *myself*, I always stumble on some particular perception or other . . . I never catch *myself* at any time without a perception, and never can observe anything but the perception" (p. 252). In the next sentence Hume draws out a consequence which must make the forlorn hope of finding the uniting principle of such a "self or person" even more forlorn: "When my perceptions are remov'd for any time, as by sound sleep; so long am I insensible of *myself*, and may truly be said not to exist." This Cartesian conclusion was one which had revolted the common sense of Locke, who harried it through ten sections of the Essay (II (i) 10-19). Heedless of those objections, Hume considers he has established that – with the possible exception of some recalcitrant metaphysicians – "the rest of mankind . . . are nothing but a bundle or collection of different perceptions, which succeed each other with an in-

conceivable rapidity, and are in a perpetual flux and movement"
(THN I (iv) 6, p. 252).

The sentence immediately following displays a truly heroic deaf-
ness to pedestrian calls for consistency (Passmore, 1952, *passim*). For
it reads: "Our eyes cannot turn in their sockets without varying our
perceptions." Noticing that "the mind is a kind of theatre, where
several perceptions successively make their appearance" although
there is "no *simplicity* in it at one time, nor *identity* in different" –
although not, it seems, noticing either the inconsistency or the crucial
relevance of his own reference to bodily organs – Hume wonders what
"gives us so great a propension to ascribe an identity to these successive perceptions, and to suppose ourselves possest of an interrupted and invariable existence thro' the whole course of our lives?"
Having ruled the obvious and right answer out of court, and having
made things still harder for himself by wantonly inserting the adjective 'invariable', he finds, somewhat surprisingly, that, "to explain
it perfectly we must take the matter pretty deep, and account for that
identity, which we attribute to plants and animals; there being a great
analogy betwixt it, and the identity of a self or person" (THN I (iv)
6, p. 253).

In developing his answer Hume assumes that we can truly and properly say that this at time one is the same such and such as that at time
two only when there has in fact between those two times been no
change at all in that particular such and such: ". . . we attribute identity, in an improper sense, to variable or interrupted objects"
(p. 255). That is, of course, a mistake: this is, or they are, perfectly
proper senses (Penelhum, 1955). Again, although he acknowledges
that we are "able to distinguish . . . betwixt numerical and specific
identity" (THN I (iv) 6, p. 257), he fails fully to come to terms with
the fact that 'same' is one of those adjectives, like 'good' and 'real',
the correct criteria for the application of which may vary with the
reference of the noun so qualified. (This was the topic of J. L. Austin's
legendary, unpublished, and perhaps never written paper, 'Goodness
and Reality'!) Making his mistaken assumption, Hume very
reasonably undertakes to review the main temptations to what he
must in consequence regard as misattributions of identity. His overriding aim "is to shew from daily experience and observation, that the
objects, which are variable and interrupted, and yet are suppos'd to
continue the same, are such only as consist of a succession of parts,

connected together by resemblance, contiguity or causation"
(p. 255).

This aim once to his own satisfaction achieved, Hume proceeds "to
explain the nature of *personal identity*, which has become so great a
question in philosophy, especially of late years in *England*, where all
the abstruser sciences are study'd with a peculiar ardour and application" (p. 259). After the *Treatise* had fallen "dead-born from the
press" Hume saw occasion to revise this patriotic judgement, thinking it too generous – especially as regards England as opposed to
Scotland. It follows, both from his more particular conclusions earlier
in the present section, and from his general principles about the
substantiality of "every distinct perception, which enters into the
composition of the mind" (p. 259), that any identity attributed to
such bundles or collections must be fictitious.

Since the unity and continuity attributed to individual human beings
is in fact about as far from fictitious as could be, Hume is quite unable
to offer any account of how we come to make a supposedly false at-
tribution without that account persistently presupposing that that at-
tribution is, after all, true. Quasi veritate coactus [as if compelled by
the truth ] he refers in his every statement either to we or to the mind
or to the imagination as reviewing or reflecting upon those successive
perceptions of which such supposedly non-substantial subjects are
supposed to consist. Thus he infers, both from his more particular recent conclusions and from his general principles, "that identity is
nothing really belonging to these different perceptions, and uniting
them together; but is merely a quality, which we attribute to them,
because of the union of their ideas in the imagination when we reflect
on them" (p. 260).

Compare also: "the transition of the mind from one object to
another" (p. 254); "The passage of the thought . . ." (p. 256); "the
mind . . . feels an easy passage from the surveying its condition in one
moment to the viewing of it in another" (p. 256); "There is, however,
another artifice, by which we may induce the imagination to advance
a step further" (p. 257); and so on.

Finally Hume seems to want us to consider the identity of other
people, rather than of ourselves: "The only question, therefore, which
remains, is, by what relations this uninterrupted progress of our
thought is produc'd, when we consider the successive existence of a
mind or thinking person" (p. 260). Here it becomes even clearer than

before that for him the master question is more scientific than philosophical. It is: neither 'What does it mean to say "same person"?' nor 'What are the correct criteria for determining whether this at time one is the same person as that at time two?'; but, rather, 'What are the psychological mechanisms which sometimes mislead us to attribute what is always in fact a fictitious identity to successive bundles or collections of perceptions?'

Hume suggests that two "relations" are responsible for "this uninterrupted progress of our thought". One is memory: in any single mind there will be later memory perceptions which must as such resemble those earlier perceptions of which they are memory images: "In this particular, then, the memory not only discovers the identity, but also contributes to its production, by producing the relation of resemblance among the perceptions" (p. 261). Presumably Hume in writing that last sentence had in mind another, which should have, yet has not, prevented any further attempts to define 'the same person as' in terms of 'remembering being the same person as'. For in his dissertation 'Of Personal Identity' the most respected of Hume's philosophical contemporaries had written: "And one should really think it self-evident, that consciousness of personal identity presupposes, and therefore cannot constitute, personal identity; any more than knowledge, in any other case, can constitute truth, which it presupposes (Butler, [1736] I, p. 388).

The other relation producing "this uninterrupted progress of our thought" is causation. As to this, "we may observe, that the true idea of the human mind, is to consider it a system of different perceptions or different existences, which are link'd together by the relation of cause and effect, and mutually produce, destroy, influence, and modify each other." Hence we can say of any particular (and conventionally male) person: "Whatever changes he endures, his several parts are still connected by the relation of causation. And in this view our identity with regard to the passions serves to corroborate that with regard to the imagination, by the making of our distant perceptions influence each other, and by giving us a present concern for our past or future pains or pleasures (THN I (iv) 6, p. 261).

All this does more to explain why questions about personal identity are important than to analyse the meanings of such questions. But Hume fires a Parthian shot, from which much philosophical profit may be gained: "The whole of this doctrine leads us to a conclusion, which is of great importance in the present affair, viz. that all the nice and subtile questions concerning personal identity can never be decided, and are to be regarded rather as grammatical than as philosophical difficulties" (p. 262). Presumably these "nice and subtile questions" are questions of the kind raised in the relevant chapter of Locke's *Essay* by various puzzle cases (II (xxvii)). And the point about such puzzle questions which needs to be taken, yet very rarely is, is, simply, that they may not have antecedently correct answers. For our present concepts were evolved in dealing with, and remain more or less well adapted to, the sorts of situations with which our ancestors were familiar. Suppose we were to be confronted by a truly unprecedented phenomenon: our spouse splits, amoeba-like, into what, albeit with some hesitations, we are inclined to call a pair of identical twins. Then we have no right, surely, to insist that there has to be, already implicit in the meanings of the relevant words, a clear-cut, unequivocally correct, yes or no answer to the question which twin, or which 'twin', we once and only once, for better or for worse, married (Flew, 1951)?

# 7

# Catastrophic Scepticism, or Merely Academic?

In the *Abstract* Hume picks out what he himself saw as the two main themes of Books I and II of the *Treatise*. In the first place, he says, the author "proposes to anatomize human nature in a regular manner . . . This treatise therefore of human nature seems intended for a system of the sciences" (p. 646). Although Hume certainly attended to the 'Rules of Reasoning in Philosophy' prefaced to Book III of the *Principia* (Newton, 1686, pp. 398-400), an earlier and more immediate inspiration to Hume's particular project for a science of human nature would seem to have been provided by Hobbes (Russell, 1985; but compare Flew, 1961, and Capaldi, 1975). Thus *The Elements of Law*, published by Hobbes in 1650, consisted of two treatises: *Human Nature*; and *de Corpore Politico*. These, along with *Of Liberty and Necessity*, reappeared in 1684 as the *Tripos*.

In the second place, however, the reports of the findings of Hume's scientific enterprise are somewhat awkwardly bound up together with discussions of a very different kind. It is difficult – indeed impossible – to reconcile these with claims to possess any sort of scientific knowledge. Hume himself concludes: "By all that has been said the reader will easily perceive, that the philosophy contain'd in this book is very sceptical . . . Our author . . . upon the whole concludes, that we assent to our faculties, and employ our reason only because we cannot help it. Philosophy wou'd render us entirely *Pyrrhonian*, were not nature too strong for it" (p. 657).

## 1 AN EVEN MORE RADICAL SCEPTICISM

Pyrrho of Elis (c. 365–275 BC) is generally regarded as the first systematic Sceptic. He seems to have believed that by suspending judgement, by confining our attention to what Hume would have called perceptions of the mind, and by eschewing assertion about what and how objects really are, we can attain not science but "impeturbable peace of mind". It is perhaps significant that Pyrrho wrote nothing. Our knowledge of his ideas, such as it is, derives in the main from the works of Sextus Empiricus (second century AD). These had a great impact following the first printing in 1569 of complete Latin translations, playing a very large part in shaping the intellectual world of Descartes (Popkin, 1964).

Already, in preceding chapters, we have seen: both that "the philosophy contain'd" in Book I is indeed "very sceptical", and that Hume's three interlocking Cartesian assumptions do indeed carry for the impossibility of knowledge implications even more drastic than those which he himself drew out. These further implications are of two kinds. In the first place, as was argued in section 3 of chapter 2, an incorporeal subject confined behind its own individual Veil of Appearance could not learn of the existence of other subjects similarly confined: those finding themselves in the predicament of epistemological solipsism could not know that there were any others in the same boat – not even if there were, or are.

The second further and even less often noticed implication is, if possible, still more catastrophic. It is that the nescience of such subjects could not be coherently and consistently expressed; or, at any rate, not in language which they could know to be, at least in principle, intelligible to others. In section 1 of chapter 2 the fundamental principle was expounded with particular reference to visual meaning. It was put then that we can only learn, and know that we have indeed correctly grasped, whatever are the established conventions for applying such purely visual terms as 'yellow' or 'red', if both we and other members of the same language-group enjoy some common access to objects in the External World correctly describable, according to the conventions of that language-group, as yellow or red. This fundamental principle can and must be generalized to embrace the thesis of what, rather mischievously, we dubbed etymological empiricism: no word can be understood by two people, and be known by them to be understood in the same sense, unless its meaning can somehow be given, and when necessary checked, by reference to their experience; and that, of course, experience in the everyday, public sense of the word.

Consider, for instance, the implication of this general principle in the particular case of two famous proposals: first, "because our senses sometimes deceive us, . . . to suppose that nothing is as they cause us to imagine it to be"; and, second, "because there are men who deceive themselves in their reasoning, and fall into paralogisms", to reject "as false all the reasonings formerly accepted as demonstrations." How could we allow that those who really were ingenuously unable to identify any performances as paradigm cases of either perception or misperception, and any arguments as either indisputably valid or inescapably invalid, were nevertheless masters of the terms in which they were thus labouring to express a near total nescience? (What, for example, should we say of the primary school teacher who gave such pupils full marks in a vocabulary test?) Yet if, on the other hand, we were to concede that such perverse nonperformers did possess the relevant linguistic competences, then we should have at once to insist that that possession necessarily presupposes – at least – that they had had, or could now acquire, some knowledge of the kinds which they were now pretending to disclaim.

Anyone who reckons to be familiar with the French national character must be wryly amused to note both the explicit and the implicit exclusions here. What Descartes outright says that he absolutley cannot doubt is his own individual existence as a being essentially conscious and essentially incorporeal. But what he never even thinks to mention is his knowledge of his cherished vernacular. (Every civilized person, surely, must know French?) But, as we have just been reminded, knowing *how* to speak that or any other natural language presupposes some knowledge *that* at least a few propositions are true (Ryle, 1949, ch. II); in particular knowledge of truths of the two kinds which Descartes wants for the moment specifically to repudiate.

The implications drawn out in sections 2 and 3 of chapter 6 are still more catastrophic. Since such basic psychological terms as 'believe', 'remember' and 'imagine' all involve some essential reference to the actual or possible behaviour of an organism, none of these could be applied to any creatures essentially incorporeal. (Flew, 1980, in addition argues that we could not coherently say even that the putative incorporeal mental substances of Platonic – Cartesian tradition might obtain information 'by telepathy' or 'by clairvoyant perception'.) It is also difficult if not impossible to suggest ways in which such supposedly hypothetical entities might be: either (before disembodiment) identified as separable from the flesh and blood persons whose minds or souls or 'selves' they are to be hypothesized as being; or (after disembodiment) reidentified as numerically the same as particular individuals, whether embodied or disembodied (Flew, 1976a, ch. 8-11).

This is not, however, the place at which to try to determine precisely what concepts, if any, they would be able to acquire and employ. For it is enough to have shown that Hume's Cartesian presuppositions do in truth demand a scepticism considerably more total than he himself ever proposed. Nevertheless it will perhaps be worthwhile simply to suggest – with all due deference both to Descartes and to so many of his successors – that and why there can be no statement even about perceptions of the mind which could not conceivably be in error. Descartes and the others, therefore, on their own Cartesian principles, ought to have doubted all their beliefs even about their own present 'thoughts'.

The best text from which to start is Locke's characteristically clear yet clearly misguided account of how language must be logically private (*Essay*, III (ii) 1-3, pp. 404-6). If only the later Wittgenstein and his associates had been willing to study such supposedly shallow classics of British philosophy they would have found here the ideal target for his critique; and the result might have been less enigmatic and more systematic than Wittgenstein, 1953. Locke proceeds, in the next chapter: "All things, that exist, being Particulars, it may perhaps be thought reasonable, that Words, which ought to be conformed to Things, should be so too, I mean in their Signification . . ." (III (iii) 1, p. 409).

In rejecting this proposition, and before going on to develop his own much criticized account 'Of General Terms', Locke somehow fails to formulate the crucial objection. Instead he first insists, quite truly, that it would be impossible to provide everything about which he might ever want to say anything with its own peculiar proper name. He goes on to point out, equally truly, both that we cannot all be directly acquainted with everything which we may wish to discuss, and that "*a distinct Name for every particular Thing, would not be of any great use for the improvement of knowledge*" (III (iii) 4, p. 410). Nevertheless, and curiously, Locke never manages to spell out the reason why it would be useless. It is, of course, that given a vocabulary consisting of nothing else but proper names we should be abundantly able to indicate possible topics of discourse, yet altogether incompetent actually to say anything about anything.

Now, uttering a proper name constitutes a kind of pointing. Any such utterance is an attempt to direct attention to the object so named. But until a proposition is made – until, that is, something is said about that object – there is nothing available to be rated as either true or false. There is nothing, therefore, either asserted or denied, either supposed or believed, either known or not known. So with reference even to the supposedly privileged perceptions of our own minds – our 'thoughts' – there is nothing either to be known or not known while these are merely being enjoyed or otherwise had, and before we have articulated some relevant assertion. (This is, presumably, what Hegel was driving at: both in refusing to admit "certainty at the level of sense-experience", or "sense-certainty", as any kind of knowledge; and in arguing that proper names must be meaningless, since the use of language proper necessarily involves some subsumption under general or universal concepts. Compare both *The Phenomenology of Mind* and, more particularly, *The Science of Logic*, I, pp. 104-5).

## 2 HUME'S EFFORTS AT CONTAINMENT

Certainly Hume, like almost everyone else, failed to appreciate the full sceptical implications of the principles which seemed to him, as to so many others, "the obvious dictates of reason", which "no man, who reflects, ever doubted" (EHU XII (i), p. 152). It is, however, equally certain that his own appreciation was already sufficient to show him that the outcome of his philosophical investigations threatened to frustrate his other intellectual and practical intentions (Passmore, 1952). The final worried section of Book I contains some of the most arresting and eloquent paragraphs in the entire *Treatise*. In the corresponding final section of the first *Enquiry* Hume returns to the problem of how and how far these drastic sceptical consequences are to be contained. Here the discussion is less dramatic. Everything appears to be under complete control. But the question remains, does Hume in the end succeed in showing that his moral science is consistent with his "very sceptical" philosophy?

. In that first final section, 'Conclusion of this book', "Methinks I am like a man, who having struck on many shoals, and having narrowly escap'd ship-wreck in passing a small frith, has yet the temerity to put out to sea in the same leaky weather-beaten vessel, and even carries his ambition so far as to think of compassing the globe under these disadvantageous circumstances." In this predicament "I am first affrighted and confounded with that forelorn solitude, in which I am plac'd in my philosophy, and fancy myself some strange uncouth monster, who not being able to mingle and unite in society, has been expell'd all human commerce, and left utterly abandon'd and disconsolate" (THN I (iv) 7, pp. 263 and 264). And so it goes on.

"For I have already shewn, that the understanding, when it acts alone, and according to its most general principles, entirely subverts itself, and leaves not the lowest degree of evidence in any proposition, either in philosophy or common life . . . For my part, I know not what ought to be done in the present case" (pp. 267-8). Nor is it only in that more particular case that Hume here confesses himself completely at a loss for any intellectual response to the various sceptical challenges presented previously. After a further brief review of these he concludes not with a decisive argument but with a decisive rejection of argument: ". . . since reason is incapable of dispelling these clouds, nature herself suffices to that purpose, and cures me of this philosophical melancholy and delirium . . . I dine, I play a game of back-gammon, I converse, and am merry with my friends; and when after three or four hours' amusement, I wou'd return to these speculations, they appear so cold, and strain'd and ridiculous, that I cannot find it in my heart to enter into them any farther" (p. 269).

Hume does not, of course, leave things at precisely that point: after all, to look no further than the *Treatise*, Book II was issued as Volume II along with Book I, and there was Book III already pressing on behind. But in the remaining pages of this final section he makes no attempt to show that any of his sceptical conclusions are in any way mistaken, whether as invalidly derived from true premises, or as validly deduced from something false. Instead he goes on to maintain that, for someone of his particular temperament and inclinations, it is on occasion equally natural to proceed with his enquiries. Notwithstanding that "If we believe, that fire warms or water refreshes, 'tis only because it costs us too much pains to think otherwise," he continues, perhaps after a refreshing interlude of back-gammon and conversation, to admit that he is "uneasy to think I approve of one object, and disapprove of another; call one thing beautiful, and another deform'd; decide concerning truth and falsehood, reason and folly, without knowing upon what principles I proceed" (p. 271).

These things once said Hume simply puts aside all his previous, ruinously sceptical conclusions. Thus, since we need some guidance in investigating subjects outside the range of "daily conversation and action", and hinting at things to come in the first *Enquiry* and the *Dialogues*, "I make bold to recommend philosophy, and shall not scruple to give it the preference to superstition of every kind or denomination" (p. 271. Then, after commending the "many honest gentlemen" of England, whom "I pretend not to make philosophers", and wishing that "we cou'd communicate to our founders of systems" some share of their down-to-earth common sense, Hume, still hoping to "contribute a little to the advancement of knowledge", turns to moral science proper: "Human Nature is the only science of man; and yet has hitherto been most neglected" (pp. 272 and 273).

For what is on this first occasion a last word, Hume recalls that he is supposed to be "very sceptical" in philosophy. But here this is construed as a matter of temperament and general approach rather than of commitment to any specific doubts and disbeliefs, however comprehensive: "A true sceptic will be diffident of his philosophical doubts, as well as of his philosophical conviction; and will never refuse any innocent satisfaction, which offers itself, upon account of either of them" (p. 273).

In Section XII of the first *Enquiry*, a work omitting some of the sceptical findings of Book I of the *Treatise*, Hume makes a more systematic effort to contain and control. His discussion 'Of the academical or sceptical Philosophy' begins by asking whether there are or could be such creatures as "*Atheists*", or "The *Sceptic* . . ., who naturally provokes the indignation of all divines and graver philosophers . . ." (EHU XII (i), p. 149). Hume thus proceeds to ask "What is meant by a sceptic?", and by so proceeding effectively sidesteps the question whether the sceptical conclusions of his own philosophizing can by any means be rendered consistent with whatever else he himself may wish to say and do.

The first "species of scepticism" which Hume recognizes here is "The Cartesian doubt", which is *antecedent* to all study and philosophy." This, as Hume rightly insists, "were it ever possible to be attained by any human creature (as it plainly is not) would be entirely incurable; and no reasoning could ever bring us to a state of assurance and conviction upon any subject" (pp. 149 and 150). But what apparently he does not notice is that it was and is precisely and only this altogether impractical and impossible "species of scepticism"which generates the three interlocking Cartesian assumptions described and distinguished in section 2 of chapter 1. Yet from these, as we shall soon be reminded, he can still see no escape.

After allowing that, understood in a more moderate sense, this first "species of scepticism" is entirely reasonable, Hume goes on to a second. This is in fact the scepticism of Book I of the *Treatise*, which was and is in fact generated from those three Cartesian assumptions. It is, he observes, "*consequent* to science and enquiry . . . Even our very senses are brought into disrepute, by a certain species of philosophers; and the maxims of common life are subjected to the same doubt as the most profound principles or conclusions of metaphysics and theology" (EHU XII (i), p. 150).

In presenting this account of "these paradoxical tenets (if they may be called tenets)" Hume sometimes suggests a certain light-hearted disrespect. Nevertheless, even as he rejects some, he still maintains that "There are other more profound arguments against the senses, which admit not of so easy a solution" (p. 151). These "more profound arguments" are the stock in trade of that "slightest philosophy, which teaches us, that nothing can ever be present to the mind but an image or perception . . ." (p. 152). In these "the profounder and more philosophical sceptics will always triumph, when they endeavour to introduce an universal doubt into all subjects of human knowledge and enquiry" (p. 153).

"There is", Hume continues, "another sceptical topic of like nature . . . which might merit our attention, were it requisite to dive so deep, in order to discover arguments and reasonings, which can so little serve to any serious purpose" (p. 154). This further topic is the distinction between primary and secondary qualities, and its introduction gives Hume an opportunity to make in a footnote one of his rare references to "Dr. Berkeley". That "his arguments, though otherwise intended, are, in reality, merely sceptical, appears from this, *that they admit of no answer, and produce no conviction*" (p. 155).

It is this suggestion of the unbelievability of sceptical conclusions which Hume develops in Part II of Section XII. They are represented as "a very extravagant attempt . . . to destroy *reason* by argument and ratiocination" (EHU XII (ii), p. 155). Here "The chief objection against all *abstract* reasonings is derived from the ideas of space and time." This objection is directed at "the doctrine of the infinite divisibility of extension" (p. 156). If only Hume had attended more closely to the notorious and formidable author of an earlier treatise on *Human Nature* he could have routed this first offensive: "For to be divided into infinite parts, is nothing else but to be divided into as many parts as any man will" (Hobbes, [1640] I, p. 63).

The second offensive in this "very extravagant attempt" launches objections against "moral evidence, or to the reasonings concerning matter of fact": these may be "either *popular* or *philosophical*" (EHU XII (ii), p. 158). It is not made clear exactly what the popular objections are, or exactly what force they are supposed to have. It is, therefore, hard to understand why Hume thinks that the response which he considers sufficient to see off the popular will not serve equally well against the philosophical: "The great subverter of *Pyrrhonism* or the excessive principles of scepticism is action, and employment, and the occupations of common life" (pp. 158-9).

Thinking as he does think, however, Hume urges that sceptics should restrict themselves to displaying "those *philosophical* objections, which arise from more profound researches", (p. 159). To no one's surprise such objections turn out to be the conclusions of Hume's own critique of arguments from experience. These Hume now proposes to confound by urging: first, that they are, as a matter of brute fact, unbelievable; and, second, that if they were for any length of time steadily believed, then the effects would be disastrous. The main interest of this proposed confounding lies in the suggestion that the position of the Pyrrhonian is somehow empty and meaningless; that, unlike those of "A Copernican or Ptolemaic", it lacks what the Logical Positivists were later to christen 'cognitive content'. Hume says: "We need only ask such a sceptic, *What his meaning is, And what he proposes by all these researches?* He is immediately at a loss, and knows not what to answer" (pp. 160 and 159-60).

All this neither is nor pretends to be a full-frontal refutation. So there is no direct inconsistency in going on to recommend "a more *mitigated* scepticism or *academical* philosophy . . . which may, in part, be the result of this Pyrrhonism . . ." (EHU XII (iii), p. 161). Such philosophy gets its name from Cicero's *Academica*. This derivative work, along with Cicero's other philosophical writings, was in Hume's century still studied as a source-book not only for the history of ideas but also for philosophy (Jones, 1982). Hume's academical scepticism here is scarcely distinguishable from the "more moderate" version of the Cartesian variety, "*antecedent* to all study and philosophy", recommended previously (EHU XII (i), pp. 150 and 149). It is effectively defined as producing that "degree of doubt, and caution, and modesty, which, in all kinds of scrutiny and decision, ought for ever to accompany a just reasoner" (EHU XII (iii), p. 162).

Finally we have what is indeed "Another species". This "*mitigated* scepticism" consists in "the limitation of our enquiries to such subjects as are best adapted to the narrow capacity of human understanding" (p. 162). The limitation required is, as we have seen, severe: "When we run over libraries, persuaded of these principles, what havoc must we make" (p. 165). The entire discussion in this concluding Section XII obscures the drastic difference: between, on the one hand, a scepticism construed as calling simply for caution, modest hesitation, and openness to correction; and, on the other hand, the positive agnosticism which denies the very possibility of knowledge, whether in some areas only or in all fields together.

## 3 A PHILOSOPHY FOR MORAL SCIENCE?

Hume clearly believes, and is clearly correct in believing, that academical scepticism is the stance appropriate to the would-be moral scientist. He is also strongly committed to insisting: both that there is no authentic knowledge to be had about anything supposedly transcending this Universe – It is, as Lord Butler might have said, the best Universe we have; and that the pressing need is to concentrate scholarly attention upon our own humankind and its affairs. "A correct Judgement", he pronounces, "confines itself to common life, and to such subjects as fall under daily practice and experience . . ." (p. 162). So far so good. But then he wants to summon Pyrrhonian scepticism to support academical: "To bring us to so salutary a determination, nothing can be more serviceable than to be once thoroughly convinced of the force of the Pyrrhonian doubt, and of the impossibility, that anything, but the strong power of natural instinct, could free us from it" (p. 162).

This, surely, will not do? For such Pyrrhonian doubt is altogether too close kin to the positive agnosticism which denies the very possibility of knowledge. In no way can such denials be rendered consistent with the erection in the areas in question of any genuine science. Hume's Pyrrhonism comprehends the whole of his External World. But instinct of course insists that "the sceptic . . . must assent to the principle concerning the existence of body, tho' he cannot pretend by any arguments of philosophy to maintain its veracity" (THN I (iv) 2, p. 187). Rather less pointedly, the same moral is drawn again in the first *Enquiry*. Yet if we cannot even know that any mind-independent objects exist, then it must be even more sure that we cannot develop any science describing the behaviour of such dubious entities.

Too many of Hume's successors have been equally complacent about this flagrant and fundamental inconsistency. For instance: in a recent general survey of his philosophy – a work which, remarkably, appears to have found no profit in any of the previous forty years of Hume literature – the distinguished author: first assures us, somewhat superfluously, that "there is no doubt that he believed in the existence of what may be called the physical objects of common sense"; and then, by ignoring the explanation quoted in our previous paragraph, concludes that Hume's immediately subsequent assertion that "'tis vain to ask, *Whether there be body or not?*" is "a cryptic statement"(Ayer, 1980, pp. 35 and 36). It is, of course, nothing of the sort. But, if we believe that it is, then we become able contentedly to ignore the objection that Hume's Pyrrhonism cannot even consist with, much less support and sustain, moral or any other kind of sciences.

If we are ever to discover fit philosophical foundations for the moral sciences, then we shall have to begin by rejecting all the three presuppositions from which that Pyrrhonism is derived. For, as has been shown in earlier chapters, the first invalidates all argument from experience, the second precludes any knowledge of mind-independent existents, while the third is nothing more nor less than a grotesque and perhaps ultimately incoherent falsehood. All three, though perennially seductive, are wildly paradoxical, both in themselves and in their consequences. This being so all of us every day of our lives are confronted with the strongest and most numerous reasons for reviewing those presuppositions, asking ourselves whether they really are inescapable. But Hume as a moral scientist had several extra and special reasons for setting himself to a radical re-examination of the third, although he himself seems never to have recognized any of these for what they were.

We noticed earlier how curious it was – and what a tribute to the tremendous impact of the *Discourse on the Method* – that Hume as a lifelong mortalist appears never to have thought to question the fundamental thesis of the Cartesian conception of the nature of man. It is equally curious that he was not similarly provoked by his equally consistent concern to show that being animals we are parts of Nature. For, although Hume lived before Darwin, he was, like Descartes, aware of the traditional Christian doctrine that individual souls, conceived as individual human essences, are separately and individually created; a doctrine which implies, and is intended to imply, an unbridgeable and categorical gulf between ourselves and the brutes. Again, his difficulties in providing accounts of the main mental concepts – particularly belief –might have, and should have, led Hume to appreciate that these all essentially involve reference to the actual and possible behaviour of organisms; and, therefore, could not by any means be applied to separable and separated Cartesian souls.

The most interesting potential stimulus, however, both because of its central philosophical importance and because of Hume's own peculiarly close involvement, is provided by his moral scientist's suggestions about how natural languages must have been evolved and acquired. For Hume was going to go on to argue, later in the *Treatise*, that these are among the many products and institutions which, although they may appear to have been designed by some Superman or God, are and must have been results of innovations and interactions between large numbers of individuals in successive generations: people none of whom were directly acquainted with most of the others who were from time to time involved; people whose actions were not and could not have been controlled from any centre; and people who would not have been capable of such achievements had they been brought together as executive committees and had these assigned to them as their collective tasks. The whole idea, therefore, of a language the terms of which all have to be defined by reference only to ideas and impressions is both psychologically and sociologically preposterous.

"Two men," Hume argues, "who pull the oars of a boat, do it by an agreement or convention, tho' they have never given promises to each other . . . In like manner are languages gradually establish'd by human conventions without any promise. In like manner do gold and silver become the common measures of exchange . . ." (III (ii) 2,

p. 490). And again, in the *Dialogues*: "If we survey a ship, what an exalted idea we must form of the ingenuity of the carpenter, who formed so complicated, useful and beautiful a machine? And what surprise must we entertain, when we find him a stupid mechanic, who imitated others, and copied an art, which, through a long succession of ages, after muliplied trials, mistakes, corrections, deliberations, and controversies, had been gradually improving?" (V, p. 167).

# 8

## Necessity, Liberty and the Possibility of Moral Science

Book II of the *Treatise* is to the modern reader, by common consent, the least rewarding. The material which Hume himself later considered fit for salvage was recycled into another examination 'Of the Passions', the only one of the *Four Dissertations* not to have been reprinted during the present century. Its latest reappearance seems to have been in the now long out of print Green and Grose edition of the *Philosophical Works of David Hume*; an edition including, unusually, the *Dialogues*. It is not even noticed in Pall Ardal's *Passion and Value in Hume's Treatise*, to which any interested reader is referred for a recent discussion of Book II. It is indeed itself remarkable only for the omission of any attempt systematically to apply the distinction between ideas and impressions or the notion of the association of ideas. For had not Hume in the *Abstract* made so bold as to hope that, "if any thing can intitle the author to so glorious a name as that of a *inventor*, 'tis the use he makes of the principle of the association of ideas" (p. 661)?

The one exception to this rule of general dreariness is provided by the first three sections of Part III. Our main business in the present chapter is with the first two, which treat 'Of liberty and necessity', a topic to which Hume returns in Section VIII of the first *Enquiry*. Both treatments, but the second more than the first, emphasize that the actual or supposed necessities which may or may not be compatible with either the reality of choice or the responsibility of agents are presuppositions both of the possibility of the moral sciences and of most of the activities of everyday life. It therefore becomes appropriate to set the scene by quoting from one of our own distinguished contemporaries, who has most consistently and persistently insisted that presuppositions of this sort are inescapable.

Thus, in a major work on *Science and Human Behaviour*, we read: "The hypothesis that man is not free is essential to the application of scientific method to the study of human behaviour" (Skinner, 1953, p. 447). The point is made again, in a more popular way, by the same author's mouthpiece in a utopian novel: "I deny that freedom exists at all. I must deny it – or my programme would be absurd. You can't have a science about a subject matter which hops capriciously about" (Skinner, 1948, ch. XXIX). Finally, in a best-selling book with the chilling title *Beyond Freedom and Dignity*, he argues in his own person: "Two features of autonomous man are particularly troublesome. In the traditional view, a person is free. He is autonomous in the sense that his behaviour is uncaused. He can therefore be held responsible for what he does, and justly punished if he offends" (Skinner, 1971, p. 19; compare Flew, 1978a, ch. 7).

## 1 A FURTHER ATTEMPT AT MENTAL MECHANICS

Psychologists such as Skinner can have little patience with endeavours to erect a science of Cartesian 'thoughts' or Humian "perceptions of the mind". In any case the work of making whatever there may be to be made of "the principle of the association of ideas" was to be much further and better advanced during Hume's own lifetime by David Hartley (1705-57). Hume himself appears to have become progressively disillusioned with this notion: several pages applying it in aesthetics were omitted from the final version of the first *Enquiry* published in 1777, with the result that what survives of Section III is the merest fragment. In the *Treatise* the one sketch for a piece of psychological science which just possibly might appeal to Skinner is the discussion of probability. In the first *Enquiry* all that remains of this is another fragment, ending: "For my part, I shall think it sufficient if the present hints excite the curiosity of philosophers and make them sensible how defective all common theories are in treating of such curious and such sublime subjects" (EHU VI, p. 59; compare Flew, 1961, pp. 105-7).

The *Treatise* devotes three whole sections to this topic; three sections which, significantly, follow immediately after four on various aspects of belief. This should give sufficient warning, if further warning be necessary, that Hume will be concerned – usually at one and the same time and without adequate discrimination – both with psychological causation and with evidential justification. So we need in our interpretation to be alert: both to the possibility that his answers to questions of one kind will be distorted by considerations relevant only to questions of the other kind; and to the fact that Hume's overriding interests are officially supposed to be scientific rather than, in our understanding, philosophical.

He distinguishes three sorts of probability, allotting one section to each: "the probability of chances"; "the probability of causes"; and "unphilosophical probability". The first case is where we know that several alternative outcomes are possible, but have no reason to think one more probable than any other: the illustration supplied is that of rolling a die. It is, Hume seems to be urging, impossible to form a belief in any one particular outcome. But of course it is not. Such irrationality is impossible only for the person of sense, "who proportions . . . belief to the evidence" (EHU X (i), p. 110).

The second case is where we have some experience of this being followed by that: "The first instance has little or no force: The second makes some addition to it: The third becomes still more sensible; and 'tis by these slow steps, that our judgement arrives at full assurance" (THN I (iii) 12, p. 130). But, alas and alack, things can never be this simple for anyone "who is arriv'd at the age of maturity"; and who has, therefore, had enough experience to be able to "build an argument on one single experiment, when duly prepar'd and examin'd." For, unfortunately, "'tis frequently found, that one observation is contrary to another" (p. 131).

Here the beliefs and practices of the vulgar appear to conflict awkwardly with those of philosophers: the latter are committed to a general doctrine of the uniformity of nature; while the former are not. Recovering himself rapidly, Hume rushes on to explain that in this case the same causes produce alternative effects: "A contrariety of events in the past may give us a kind of hesitating belief in the future after two several ways" (p. 132). Suppose, for example, that "I have found by long observation, that of twenty ships, which go to sea, only nineteen return." And suppose too that "I see that at present . . . twenty ships leave the port" (p. 134). Then the result, Hume seems to be saying, may be: either "a kind of hesitating belief" that they will all return; or a more robust confidence that nineteen out of the original twenty will make it safely.

In the remainder of section 12 Hume is in the main concerned, quite frankly and explicitly, not with matters of putative fact, but with questions of "Just reasoning" (p. 135). Nevertheless there is also one delightful piece of high psychological theorizing. It concludes: "Thus a man, who desires a thousand pound, has in reality a thousand or more desires, which uniting together, seem to make only one passion; tho' the composition evidently betrays itself upon every alteration of the object, by the preference he gives to the larger number, if superior only by an unite" (p. 141). If you are unable to relish this, then – as Hume was to say in a rather different connection – "you need only conclude that your turn of mind is not suited to the moral sciences" (EPM App. I, p. 289).

Section 12 concludes with an inadequate explanation of a third sort of probability "arising from ANALOGY" (THN I (iii), p. 142). The next begins: "All these kinds of probability are receiv'd by philosophers, and allow'd to be reasonable foundations of belief and opinion. But there are others, that are deriv'd from the same principles, tho' they have not had the good fortune to obtain the same sanction" (I (iii) 13, p. 143). This is, presumably, Hume's way of announcing that he will now proceed to distinguish various unsound forms of argument from experience. By putting it in this way he discourages questions: both about the principles, if any, which legitimate these grantings and withdrawals of endorsement; and about how, if all belief is causally necessitated, anyone's thinking is ever to be improved (Flew, 1961, pp. 98-9).

But, whether although or because such radical queries have been ruled out of order, Hume here is very much the future historian rather than the Pyrrhonian philosopher. For instance: he entertains an argument that the very length of the causal chains linking us today to events in the remote past will or should eventually dispel any conviction that those events did actually occur. (It is a curious argument,which has been traced back to John Craig, a friend of Newton. In 1699 Craig's *Theologiae Christianae Principia Mathematica* apparently estimated that the Gospels would lose all credibility by AD 3150!) Hume slaps all this down very smartly: "There is no variation in the steps . . . This circumstance alone preserves the evidence of history, and will perpetuate the memory of the present age to the latest posterity" (THN I (iii) 13, p. 146).

The most interesting of these "unphilosophical species of probability" is the fourth. This is "deriv'd from *general rules*, which we rashly form to ourselves, and which are the source of what we properly call PREJUDICE" (p. 146). Hume sees general rules, both good and bad, as extremely important, not only in theoretical matters but also in practical affairs. "For," as he goes on to say much later, "there is a principle of human nature, . . . that men are mightily addicted to *general rules*, and that we often carry our maxims beyond those reasons, which first induc'd us to establish them" (THN III (ii) 9, p. 551).

Here in section 13 he promises that in section 15 he will provide us with those 'Rules by which to judge of causes and effects' which, as was said earlier, anticipate Mill's Four Methods of Experimental Inquiry (p. 149). It is unfortunate that by confining attention to the possible causes of and warrants for affirmative belief, Hume leaves no room for first entertaining and then testing some generalization, before becoming categorically committed either to its truth or to its falsity. For – properly – a prejudice is not a tentative conjecture but a firm belief; and as such to be condemned neither as of necessity false nor as personally favoured, but as reached prior to investigation (Flew, 1975, §§ 1.55-6 and 5.6).

## 2 TWO BITES AT THE CHERRY

In his discussion 'Of liberty and necessity' in the *Treatise* Hume denounces "the doctrine of liberty" as "fantastical" ': it is "absurd . . . in one sense, and unintelligible in any other" (II (iii) 1 and 2, pp. 407, 404 and 407). Both his reasons and his vehemence would commend him to Skinner. But in the first *Enquiry*, under exactly the same heading, Hume presents a "reconciling project" with regard to "the most contentious question of metaphysics, the most contentious science" (VIII (i), p. 95). Despite this striking difference of tone and temper the substance of both treatments is very similar.

In both, Hume starts from the necessities which, he contends, are both presupposed and discovered not only by the moral sciences but also in everyday life; although he does in both eventually go on to notice theological implications of conclusions about what is for him the primary problem. In both, Hume sees his contribution as a corollary of findings from the investigation of causation: "Our author pretends", as the *Abstract* has it, "that this reasoning puts the whole controversy in a new light, by giving a new definition of necessity" (p. 661). Certainly, what he said was new. But we cannot protest either too soon or too often that what Hume is really offering is in truth: not so much a new account of the meaning of the word 'necessity'; as, rather, a denial that there is any such thing as that to which that word, as previously understood, pretended to refer. Persistent and reiterated protest is required. For Hume himself, here and elsewhere, constantly employs both that particular word and various semantic associates in senses far stronger than anything for which he is officially prepared to provide.

(i) Thus, in the *Treatise*, after explaining that "by the *will*" he means "*the internal impression*" which we have when we do something, Hume attends to the "universally acknowledg'd" necessities of physics. "The actions . . . of matter", he continues, "are to be regarded as instances of necessary actions; and whatever is in this respect on the same footing with matter must be acknowledg'd to be necessary." Living before the era of quantum mechanics, Hume was not inhibited against asserting that "Every object is determin'd by an absolute fate to a certain degree and direction of its motion . . ." (II (iii) 1, pp. 399 and 400). All this is entirely fair and wholly to the point. Certainly, whatever is in this respect on the same footing with matter must be acknowledged to be subject to what earlier – in chapter 5 above – was distinguished as practical or causal necessity. But that, of course, involves bonds far stronger than anything compassed by Hume's proposed "new sense of necessity".

No one, however, has any business either not to notice or to be surprised that, when Hume forthwith sets himself to demonstrate that human action is subject to the same inexorable necessity, what he in fact attempts, and considers that he succeeds in doing, is much more modest. It is to argue only that there are everywhere to be discovered universal and reliable regularities. What Hume actually does is, surely, well worth doing? For it is important to bring out that there are sufficient and sufficiently universal regularities in actual human behaviour for both moral science and social life to be possible; even if it has not been shown, and perhaps cannot be, that completely true, universal generalizations are possible everywhere.

Be that as it may. What is beyond dispute is that Hume cannot by these means hope to prove, what even if it were true could not be established in this way, that all the actual movements of human beings are as inexorably necessitated as the movements of the planets and the stars; that none of us ever are more able than they to depart from those various lines, precise or imprecise, in which we move. This being so, Hume's corollary conclusions are left hanging in the air. He has not, therefore, as he hoped and believed, disposed of "the doctrine of liberty". That here, as he explains rather by the way, is liberty in the second sense: "Few are capable of distinguishing betwixt the liberty of *spontaniety*, as it is call'd in the schools, and the liberty of *indifference*; betwixt that which is oppos'd to violence, and that which means a negation of necessity and causes" (II (iii) 2, p. 407).

(ii) The reconciliation negotiated in the first *Enquiry* instead interprets liberty in the first of these two ways. Hume is thus following in the Compatibilist tracks of Hobbes. In chapter XXI of his *Leviathan* Hobbes wrote: "*Liberty*, or *freedom* signifieth, properly, the absence of opposition; by *opposition* I mean external impediments of motion . . ." In this understanding, in order to effect a reconciliation, it is not even required that "a new definition of necessity" be introduced. For it remains possible that, without having been constrained by any "external impediments of motion", someone might have been causally necessitated to behave in this one particular manner and no other. As Hume himself says, "this hypothetical liberty is universally allowed to belong to everyone who is not a prisoner and in chains" (EHU VIII (i), p. 95). It may, we may add, be similarly allowed to belong even to bits of inanimate mechanism; where these are truly said, in so far as their movements are not physically obstructed, to be free to move.

The question arises, therefore, why Hume thought that the introduction of "a new definition of necessity" made a crucial difference? The answer is that what, with some reason, Hume called "the most contentious question of metaphysics, the most contentious science" is misrepresented as a problem about liberty as opposed to constraint. For the truth is that it is a problem about agency and choice. On the factual side the question is whether we are often or ever, as agents, in situations where we have, in some strong sense, a choice; and then choose to do this when we could alternatively have done either that or the other. (The expression 'in some strong sense' has to be there in order to rule out as irrelevant the reply that what we have just heard Hume describing as "this hypothetical liberty" is indeed universally allowed to belong to everyone who is not a prisoner and in chains.) On the philosophical side the questions are: 'What would be logically presupposed and logically implied by such factual claims?'; and 'What are the senses in which the various key terms are being employed?'

Once it is appreciated that the real problem is a problem about choice, it becomes obvious why Hume thinks that "a new definition of necessity" is relevant; and obvious too that he is right so to think. For choice either is, or involves, or at any rate looks very like, what in the *Treatise* Hume execrated as "the liberty of *indifference*; which means a negation of necessity and causes." But now, given that new definition, and given too that in human affairs also necessity rules, no sense of liberty involving "a negation of necessity and causes" can find any application there.

Certainly, if I were always causally necessitated to behave in whatever turn out to be the ways in which I do in fact behave, then it could not also be the case that sometimes I could, in some suitably strong sense, have behaved in some fashion other than that in which I actually did behave. It is because Skinner believes, both that all human behaviour is so caused, and that any psychological science must presuppose that that is so, that he has to deny: both "that freedom exists"; and that anyone can properly "be held responsible for what he does, and justly punished if he offends."

Suppose, on the other hand, that there is, after all, no such thing as causal necessity. Suppose that the cash value of so much talk misleading us to believe the opposite is no more than that of a pile of propositions reporting mere constant conjunctions and brute facts about regular succession. Then, it seems, the scientist ceases to be committed to denying any contentions cherished in "the literature of dignity" (Skinner, 1971, p. 55).

Allowing that nothing necessitates the senses of choices, moral scientists may still become able, more often than the rest of us, to predict how people will behave, and even in what senses they will choose. But this in itself will have no tendency to show that such choices will not really be choices, and that the chooser could not have chosen otherwise. For there is a world of difference: between, on the one hand, knowing that someone will in fact act thus and thus; and,

on the other hand, knowing that they are – willy nilly – necessitated
so to behave.

This crucial difference is most elegantly displayed, in a theological
context, by the Renaissance Humanist Lorenzo Valla. (It was he who,
as a Papal Secretary, first demonstrated that the *Donation of Constantine*
is a forgery!) Valla's *Dialogue on Freewill*, mediated perhaps through
Bayle or Leibniz, was very probably Hume's ultimate source for the
suggestion that we are all apt here to be misled by what Popper has
christened the Oedipus Effect (Popper, 1957, p. 13). What in the
*Treatise* is scarcely so much as a hint becomes in the first *Enquiry* a full
footnote (VII (i), p. 94).

(iii) In the earlier work, while protesting that opinions are not proved
to be false by demonstrations of their dangerous consequences, Hume
ventures "to affirm, that the doctrine of necessity, according to my explanation of it, is not only innocent, but even advantageous to
religion and morality" (II (iii) 2, p. 409). But later he sees and
exploits an opportunity to draw out morals congenial to the whole
enterprise of the first *Enquiry*: "To reconcile the indifference and contingency of human actions with prescience; or to defend absolute
decrees, and yet free the Deity from being the author of sin, has been
found hitherto to exceed all the power of philosophy. Happy, if she be
thence sensible of her temerity, . . . and . . . return, with suitable
modesty, to her true and proper province, the examination of common life" (VIII (ii), p. 103).

Hume's whole enterprise in Part II of Section VIII is, however,
fundamentally flawed. Very reasonably, he insists first that all reward
and punishment must presuppose that the persons to be so treated are
the causes of whatever it is for which they are to be rewarded or
punished. (Not so reasonably, and entirely by the way, he appears further to require that their actions be in character – p. 98.) Hume then
entertains what ironically he presents as an objection "to this theory
with regard to necessity and liberty . . . It may be said, for instance,
that if voluntary actions be subjected to the same laws of necessity
with the operations of matter, there is a continued chain of necessary
causes, pre-ordained and pre-determined, reaching from the original
cause of all to every single volition of every human creature" (p. 99).
Thus, Hume continues, speaking of God, "He foresaw, he ordained,
he intended all those actions of men which we so rashly pronounce

criminal. And we must, therefore, conclude either that they are not criminal or that the Deity, not man, is accountable for them" (p. 100).

Of these two options Hume rules out the first on what is for him the congenial, radically secular and humanist ground that "these distinctions are founded in the natural sentiments of the human mind . . . not to be controlled or altered by any philosophical theory or speculation whatsoever" (p. 103). The second is therefore chosen. But it is construed as justifying the equally congenial, equally secular moral that philosophy should confine herself to the proper province of the human understanding, the study of human nature and human affairs, "without launching into so boundless an ocean of doubt, uncertainty and contradiction" (p. 103).

What even those interpreters who appreciated Hume's irony have failed to recognize is that this pretended objection both in fact and necessarily construes causation in a much stronger sense than any for which he can make provision (Flew, 1961, pp. 159-65; but compare Flew, 1978b). Thus the penultimate passage quoted in the last paragraph but one has to continue, immediately: "No contingency anywhere in the universe, no indifference, no liberty. While we act, we are at the same time acted upon. The ultimate Author of all our volitions is the Creator of the world, who first bestowed motion on this immense machine and placed all beings in that particular position whence every subsequent event, by an inevitable necessity, must result" (pp. 99-100).

We categorically cannot read this talk of "an inevitable necessity" in Hume's official, denatured sense. For liberty, as he has himself been arguing in Part I, is completely compatible with necessity, in "a new sense of necessity". But in the present passage Divine causality specifically leaves no room whatsoever for alternatives, "no liberty". So what in Part II is supposed to be the particular application of the reconciling ideas of Part I is in fact inconsistent with them. The objection with which Hume, as an aggressive agnostic, hopes to devastate theism must itself collapse if Hume's account of causation is correct. But if that account is to be accepted in its entirety, then theists too must be involved in a common ruin.

` The crux is that the notion of agency, whether human or Divine, itself contains and implies much more than that brute fact constant conjunction and mere succession which is all which Hume can admit into causation as a philosophical relation. In the *Abstract* he concludes, in a picturesque trope, that the principles of the association of ideas "are really *to us* the cement of the universe" (p. 662). But for him the corollary is and must be that the Universe *in itself*, outwith the human mind, has no cement at all; everything is "entirely loose and separate".

Doing, however, is a kind of causing, of making something happen. Such a Humian a universe will, therefore, be one in which nothing at all is ever actually done. Nothing happens, that is to say, such that something else would not have happened if that had not. Nothing is ever made either practically impossible or practically inevitable, whether by human agency or by God. There just are only universal regularities in the occurrence of events in themselves entirely loose, separate and unconnected.

So Hume is not on this account entitled to help himself to that comfortable teaching against "launching into so boundless an ocean of doubt, uncertainty, and contradiction." If the theologians were to accept Hume's reductive reinterpretation of the necessity of causes, then they could spare their God the charge of being the ultimate author of sin. But then they, like the rest of us, would benefit from that reductive reinterpretation only at the altogether unacceptable price of maintaining that no one, whether God or man, actually brings about anything at all!

### 3 CHOICE AND POWER

"Hume's main object . . . is to show that the moral sciences can be established on a secure footing" (Passmore, 1952, p. 15). This claim, though intended by its maker to have a much wider scope, is true particularly of Hume's discussions both 'Of liberty and necessity' and 'Of the Idea of necessary Connexion'. Like Skinner, and like so many others too, Hume saw "the liberty of *indifference*" as prejudicing the possibility of moral science. Hume and Skinner are also verbally agreed in their insistence that all the behaviour even of human beings, as well as all the behaviour of inanimate objects, is determined by the same absolute causal necessity. Where they differ, of course, is in their interpretations of the key words in their agreement. Hume's conclusion in the *Treatise* is "that there is but one kind of necessity, as there is but one kind of cause, and that the common distinction betwixt *moral* and *physical* necessity is without any foundation in nature" (I (iii) 14, p. 171).

Later, in the essay 'Of National Characters', he does want to make a distinction between physical and moral causes. This is at the same time a distinction between the subject materials with which the physical and the moral sciences are concerned: "By *moral* causes, I mean all circumstances, which are fitted to work on the mind as motives or reasons . . . By *physical* causes I mean those qualities of the air and climate, which are supposed to work insensibly on the temper, by altering the tone and habit of the body . . ." (p. 198). Hume did not, however, anticipate Weber and his successors by arguing that explanations in terms of these two different kinds of cause are of two irreducibly different logical types (Flew, 1985, ch. 2). Where he did anticipate the other Scottish founding fathers of social science by several years was in his emphatic appreciation of the crucial importance for the social sciences of the unintended consequences of intended action (Hayek, 1967, ch. 5-7, and Hayek, 1978, ch. 15-16). Thus Hume concludes his essay 'Of Taxes' by observing that these provide "an instance of what frequently happens in political institutions, that the consequences of things are diametrically opposite to what we should expect on the first appearance" (p. 347).

By maintaining that "the common distinction betwixt *moral* and *physical* necessity is without any foundation in nature" Hume disqualified himself from discerning, and discriminating between, two corresponding senses of 'cause'. Yet there is an absolutely fundamental difference: between, on the one hand, ensuring that some person will act in one particular way by providing them with some overwhelmingly strong reason so to do; and, on the other hand, making some purely physical phenomenon happen by bringing about the causally sufficient conditions of its occurence. That absolutely fundamental difference is that, whereas such sufficient physical causes necessarily necessitate the occurrence of their effects, correspondingly sufficient moral causes do not. If, for instance, I convey to you some splendid news – news which, if you decided to celebrate, you and everyone else would point to as the cause of that celebration – then I do not by so doing ensure that you must, willy-nilly, make whoopee.

In his reconciliation 'Of Liberty and Necessity' Hume is considering "the liberty of *spontaneity*." He is, therefore, committed to construing statements that his agents could have done otherwise as implying only that they are not in straightjackets. His contributions to examining claims that it must be in some much stronger sense that as agents we are normally, indeed necessarily, able to do otherwise come in discussions not 'Of Liberty and Necessity' but 'Of the Idea of necessary Connexion'; and with particular reference to the notion of power. Thus in the *Treatise* we have only one curt, crushing single-sentence paragraph – immediately following that of the previous quotation: "The distinction, which we often make betwixt *power* and the *exercise* of it, is equally without foundation" (p. 171).

Perhaps it is less than instantly obvious what this most categorical statement is supposed to be denying. But some light is to be found in the rather unexpected context of a discussion 'Of property and riches'. Here, after reiterating that the distinction aforesaid "is entirely frivolous", Hume nevertheless allows that, "tho' this be strictly true in a just and *philosophical* way of thinking, 'tis certain it is not *the philosophy* of our passions" (II (i) 10, p. 311). The upshot is: "Since therefore we ascribe a power of performing an action to every one, who has no very powerful motive to forbear it, and refuse it to such as have; it may justly be concluded, that *power* has always a reference to its *exercise*, either actual or probable, and that we consider a person as endow'd with any ability, when we find from past experience, that 'tis probable, or at least possible that he may exert it" (p. 313).

What we need here is another very important and fundamental distinction; a distinction between, if you like, a physical and a moral or personal power. Physical powers are possessed by or attributed to inanimate objects; and powers of this kind are definable, as Hume urges, in terms of the actual or possible behaviour of those objects to which they are attributed. This is the sense in which one speaks of the brake horsepower of a car, or of the explosive power of what at one time was rather prissily known as 'a nuclear device'. The second sense, the sense in which Hume in the *Treatise* wanted to deny that there is any such thing, is that of personal power. It is in this understanding that it might be unfashionably said that J. V. Stalin possessed the power of life or death – or much worse – over every single subject of what we should nowadays be reproached for describing as his evil empire. Failure to make and maintain this distinction was responsible for much of the confusion in, and between, and arising from, the *First Essay* and the *Second Essay* of Malthus (Flew, 1984, ch. 4; and compare Flew, 1978a ch. 2).

To possess such personal power is to be able, at will, either to have or to do what it is the power to have or to achieve. Whatever people possessing such personal power choose to do, it has to be true too that, in some strong sense, they could have done otherwise. In order to achieve a better understanding, both of what that sense is and of why Hume denied that it could have any reference we need to make another, more flexible and more constructive review of the great chapter 'Of Power' in Locke's *Essay*. Certainly Hume makes it very clear that it is primarily this document which he is criticizing in both his treatments 'Of the Idea of necessary Connexion'.

It is unfortunate that in these critiques Hume does not let Locke speak for himself. Speaking for him Hume proposes: "It may be said, that we are every moment conscious of internal power; while we feel, that by the simple command of our will, we can move the organs of our body, or direct the faculties of our mind . . . This influence of the will we know by consciousness" (EHU VII (ii), p. 64). The nub of Hume's objection is put in the single sentence: "This influence, we may observe, is a fact, which like all other natural events, can be known only by experience, and can never be foreseen from any apparent energy or power in the cause, which connects it with the effect, and renders the one an infallible consequence of the other" (pp. 64-65).

To understand both the objection itself, and why the answer provided is believed to be decisive, we have to recognize that both challenge and response take our three Cartesian presuppositions for granted. This recognition is handicapped by the inclusion of an unsceptical reference to knowledge in the definition of 'will' in the *Treatise*: "I desire it may be observ'd, that by the *will*, I mean nothing but the *internal impression we feel and are conscious of, when we knowingly give rise to any new motion of our body, or new perception of our mind.*" Hume underlines his intention to refer to a supposed impression – a kind of Cartesian 'thought', such as might be had by an incorporeal subject of consciousness – by adding at once: "This impression . . . 'tis impossible to define, and needless to describe any farther . . ." (II (iii) 1, p. 399). But, by the first of the three Cartesian principles, the having of such a 'thought' cannot constitute a sufficient ground for claims to know the consequences thereof. So the insertion of the expression "knowingly give rise" is another of Hume's deplorably characteristic inconsistencies (Passmore, 1952).

Suppose now that we look for ourselves at how Locke tried to explain the notion of power. Certainly he too was handicapped by the same Cartesian presuppositions. But if we are not, then we can find

Locke's contribution most helpfully suggestive. At first his words are very like those which Hume puts into his mouth: "This at least I think evident, That we find in our selves a *Power* to begin or forbear, continue or end several actions of our minds, and motions of our Bodies, barely by a thought or preference of the mind ordering, or as it were command the doing or not doing such or such a particular action. This *power* is that which we call the *Will*" (II (xxi) 5, p. 236).

Soon, however, it is a different and better story; marred only by the fact that Locke sees himself as spelling out what is meant by 'a free agent' rather than, more simply and more fundamentally, by 'an agent' or – And, surely, tautologically? – 'a choosing agent'. The three Latin words refer to St. Vitus's dance: "Every one, I think, finds in himself a *Power* to begin or forbear . . . We have instances enough, and often more than enough in our own Bodies. A Man's Heart beats, and the Blood circulates, which 'tis not in his Power . . . to stop; and therefore in respect of these Motions, where rest depends not on his choice . . . he is not a *free Agent*. Convulsive Motions agitate his Legs, so that though he wills it never so much, he cannot . . . stop their Motion, (as in that odd Disease called *chorea Sancti Viti*,) but he is perpetually dancing. He is . . . under as much Necessity of moving, as a Stone that falls, or a Tennis-ball struck with a Racket. On the other side, a Palsie or the Stocks hinder his Legs . . ." (II (xxi) 7 and 11, pp. 237 and 239).

Locke has in this seminal passage shown that and how it is possible to provide ostensive definitions, not only of '(personal) power' but all the other key terms and expressions also – terms and expressions such as '(choosing) agent', '(practical) necessity', or 'can (in a strong sense) do other than they do do'. It seems too that no one could ever be in a position consistently to assert, much less to know: either that there is no such thing as unnecessitated choice; or that there is no such thing as practical necessity. For it appears that choice and necessity are two opposites of such a kind that each can be explained only by pointing to actual specimens both of its own and of the other sort. Thus anyone able to understand either of these two notions must have been acquainted with some specimens of both the two sorts of realities to which they respectively refer.

This is not a contention which it is either possible or necessary fully to establish here. It will be sufficient first simply to indicate that it does at least have considerable plausibility; and then to challenge doubters to falsify it, if they can, by developing ways of explaining these notions which do not involve and require such complementary ostension. If indeed it cannot be falsified, for the sufficient reason that it is true, then Hume's work will have to be seen as providing the strongest classical support for that truth. In chapter 7 it was argued that his failure to answer the question how persons conceived as incorporeal are to be reidentified through time should be turned round, and re-employed to support the thesis that there is no room in logical space for a coherent concept of bodiless personal existence. The parallel suggestion here is that Hume's failure to find any basis in experience, conceived in his Cartesian terms, for the ideas of either practical necessity or "the liberty of *indifference*" should also be constructively re-employed; this time to sustain the contention that these ideas are and can be acquired only through our ordinary acquaintance, as flesh and blood agents, with the corresponding realities. (This is a finding of which all those not yet emancipated from Hume's three Cartesian presuppositions deprive themselves; compare Popper, 1982.)

In order to show how the argument must go, we have to insist on starting not with Lockean ideas or Humian "perceptions of the mind" but with bodily movements. Let those which can be either initiated or quashed at will be labelled 'movings', and those which cannot 'motions'. (These recommendations have the merit of going with rather than against the grain of common usage.) Certainly it is obvious that there are plenty of marginal cases. Nevertheless, so long as there are, as there are, plenty – indeed, far, far more – which fall unequivocally upon one side or the other, we must resolutely and stubbornly refuse to be prevented from insisting on a humanly vital distinction by any such diversionary appeals to the existence of marginal cases.

Now suppose that, for the moment, and for the sake of simplicity: we both ignore purely mental actions – such as summoning up a mental image; and refuse to make any distinction between those cases in which an agent chooses to move and those in which the choice is *not* to move. Then it becomes easy to recognize that the notions of action, of choice and (in the strong sense) of being able to do otherwise can be, and surely must be, explained by reference to what, given the previous simplifying assumptions, all actions must involve; namely, movings as distinct from motions. It also becomes, and this time without requiring any simplifying assumptions, easy to appreciate that all of us as agents are forever engaged in confronting ourselves with both practical necessities and their complementary practical impossibilities; and that is by no means only or primarily in attempting to control some of our own bodily motions.

How then is it that in his discussions 'Of the Idea of necessary Connexion' Hume fails to discover any fully legitimating source? There are two reasons. In the first place, his overriding concern is to defend the insight that, "If we reason *a priori*, anything may appear able to produce anything" (EHU XII (iii), p. 164). So he never clearly recognizes the possibilities of a second sense of 'necessity'; of a second sort of necessity. In the second place, Hume's whole investigation is conducted within the framework provided by his three Cartesian presuppositions. So, trying to act as if he were an incorporeal subject of purely private experience, he searches for the impression from which a not specifically practical idea of necessary connection might have been derived. Then, by appealing to the first of his three Cartesian principles, all the few candidates presenting themselves for examination are promptly disqualified. For it must remain always conceivable that the having of any particular candidate impression will in fact be followed by some occurrence other than whatever its actual practical consequence is believed to be.

The nearest that Hume comes to seeking some source for the idea of "the liberty of *indifference*" is when he puts it down, in part at least, to "*religion*, which has been very unnecessarily interested in this question" (THN II (iii) 2, p. 409). Instead he argues that, because it "means a negation of necessity and causes" (p. 407), it must be either a pseudo-concept or a concept without any actual objects. In particular, mainly in the discussions 'Of Liberty and Necessity', but also elsewhere, Hume argues that we find a same universal causal determinism and the same universal causal necessity everywhere. They are both presupposed and discovered, not only in and by the moral sciences, but also in the practical business of everyday living.

Properly understood, however, none of this constitutes any reason to deny the reality of choice. Instead it can, given such understanding, be turned round to supply reasons for denying that any such denial is necessary. To effect this salutary and constructive reversal we need: first, to remind ourselves of the distinction, developed earlier in the present section 3, between two senses of the word 'cause' – the one necessitating and the other not; and then, that done, we need to continue the same discrimination in order to distinguish two corresponding senses of 'determinism', or sorts of determinism. With one sort the claim of the determinist becomes that all occurrences, other than actions, are determined by necessitating causes; while with the other it is that all actions are determined by motivating reasons – by wants or desires or other reasons for action which, in a phrase borrowed from Leibniz, "incline but do not necessitate".

Certainly this carries the implication that the senses of human actions cannot be determined by necessitating laws of nature; although, given that people have acted thus or thus, the consequences may still be practically necessary. But a denial of complete necessitating causal determinism does not in its turn imply that the moral sciences have "a subject matter which hops capriciously about". For, remembering that by 'necessity' in such contexts Hume is supposed to mean only regularity, considerations of the kind which Hume urged can be redeployed to demonstrate that the behaviour of that human subject matter is by no means wholly capricious and unpredictable.

On the contrary: both moral scientists and laypersons frequently possess adequate reasons for predicting the senses of particular human actions; and, even where prediction was not in practice possible, they may still, after the event, for the most excellent reasons given, insist that certain agents 'had no choice' or 'could not have done otherwise'. It is as important as it is uncommon to point out that these expressions are ordinarily and correctly uttered only when and where the speakers can be confident that, in a more literal understanding, the agents did have a choice and – precisely because and in so far as they were agents – could (in the strong sense) have done other than they did. What is meant by these idioms is that there was, whether in the descriptive or the prescriptive sense of 'expect', no available alternative course of action which they could reasonably be expected to take (Flew, 1978a, ch. 2-4 and 7-9).

The case, for instance, of the recalcitrant businessman, receiving from *The Godfather* 'an offer which he cannot refuse', is vitally different from that of the errant mafioso, who is without warning gunned down from behind. The former is an agent, however reluctant. But the latter, in that very moment of sudden death, ceases to be. He, in the most literal understanding, has no choice. But the unfortunate businessman does have; even though the alternative to acceptance is perhaps even more intolerable: 'In thirty seconds from now I propose to have on this paper either your signature or your brains!'

# 9

## Values as Socially Projected

Psychoanalysts have long been notorious for refusing to allow even the most compelling external evidence to upset the interpretations emerging from their analytic hours. Occasionally some of the less scholarly students of Hume's writings have displayed an equally resolute reluctance to refer to biographical materials. The most grotesque results of this perverse self-denying ordinance have been attempts to make out that in the *Dialogues* Cleanthes or Demea, rather than Philo, comes nearest to expressing Hume's own conclusions. In the published discussions of questions about values there is no corresponding difficulty in disentangling the author's own convictions from the inhibitions of discretion. Yet by looking at the biographical background we can learn something more about the road by which Hume came to his conclusions, and what he saw as most important.

To the question whether he was a Pyrrhonian sceptic or a scientific naturalist, the true answer is, surely, that he was both; that to the end he continued to alternate between these inconsistents? That this was indeed so is made plain by what seems to have been the final footnote added to the *Dialogues* (XII, p. 219; and compare Chappell, 1966, pp. 97-8). A similar answer should be given to the question whether Hume first approached philosophy by way of religion or of morality. Kemp Smith contended: "that it was through the gateway of morals that Hume entered into his philosophy" (p. vi); and that it was chiefly the recently published works of Hutcheson which, when he "was about 18 Years of Age . . . open'd up . . . a new Scene of Thought . . ." (Greig, 1932, I, p. 13). More recently Mossner has remarked, truly, that "Religion . . . was one of the dominant interests of Hume throughout his life", suggesting that "the intense interest of the schoolboy in religion . . . impelled the youth into the paths of philosophy" (Mossner, 1977, p. 2).

That these two apparently opposed concerns were in Hume's case complementary and mutually reinforcing will scarcely surprise those who themselves reached those paths by much the same route. That such a route is both possible and likely can be seen by considering the last paragraph of the letter in which Hume solicited the help of Hutcheson in arranging for the publication of Book III of the *Treatise*: "I wish from my Heart, I coud avoid concluding, that since Morality, according to your Opinion as well as mine, is determin'd merely by Sentiment, it regards only human Nature and human Life . . . the Consequences are very momentous." The one which Hume proceeds to draw is that moral qualities can neither be derived from nor attributed to Deity: "If Morality were determined by Reason, that is the same for all rational Beings: But nothing but Experience can assure us that the Sentiments are the same. What Experience have we with regard to superior Beings? How can we ascribe to them any Sentiments at all?" (Greig, 1932, I, p. 40).

Hume's fundamental conclusion is that value characteristics in general, and moral in particular, are a sort of secondary qualities. Things in themselves actually possess certain primary qualities which, because we are the kind of creatures we are, cause us to react in certain ways. We then project these valuing reactions out onto what in truth possesses no value, whether positive or negative. This main point is most persuasively put in Appendix I to the second *Enquiry*: most of what in the narrow modern sense we should rate as philosophy is in that "bland and insipid document" is relegated to four appendices (Penelhum, 1975, p. 37). "Euclid," Hume asserts, "has fully explained all the qualities of the circle; but has not in any proposition said a word of its beauty. The reason is evident. The beauty is not a quality of the circle . . . It is only the effect which that figure produces upon the mind, whose peculiar fabric or structure renders it susceptible of such sentiments" (EPM, pp. 291-2).

This fundamental conclusion could just as well have been reached first in thinking about either religion or morality. Whichever it was, Hume, almost equally interested in both, was bound to apply it at once to the other. On the one hand, it enables him to develop what became for the modern period the first completely secular and humanist account of morality. On the other hand, it gives him a powerful critical weapon, especially effective against the theology of Butler's *Analogy* – Butler being the one contemporary Christian apologist for whom, very properly, Hume had a real respect (Stephen, 1876, ch. V–VI).

Before proceeding we should perhaps emphasize that it was Hume himself who first drew out the analogy between this account of value characteristics and the account of secondary qualities to be found in Galileo, Newton and others. It was indeed Hume's observation of such similarities, both in this case and in that of his account of causal necessity, which raised his confidence that the introduction of "the experimental method of reasoning into moral subjects" was on sound lines and yielding good fruit. This point apparently needs to be stressed, since one of those recent books designed to fill a Hume-shaped gap in a series makes a patronizing suggestion: "Hume's aims would be served by a theory of moral judgements that follows the same general lines as I suggested for the case of necessity . . . In that way virtue and vice are like secondary qualities . . ." (Stroud, 1977, p. 184).

There is absolutely no call here for the contribution of kindly crutches. For Hume makes the point himself, with characteristic force and clarity, and in the very paragraph upon which this superfluous suggestion was offered as a comment: "Vice and virtue, therefore, may be compar'd to sounds, colours, heat and cold, which, according to modern philosophy, are not qualities in objects, but perceptions in the mind: And this discovery in morals, like that other in physics, is to be regarded as a considerable advancement of the speculative sciences; tho', like that too, it has little or no influence on practice" (THN III (i) 1, p. 469; and compare Kemp Smith, 1941, p. 19).

It was upon the foundation of "this discovery" that Hume attempted to construct a psychology of morals. The prospectus for this enterprise in the first *Enquiry* is part of the triumphant concluding survey of all academically respectable subjects: "Morals and criticism are not so properly objects of the understanding as of taste and sentiment. Beauty, whether moral or natural, is felt more properly than perceived. Or if we reason concerning it, and endeavour to fix its standard, we regard a new fact, to wit, the general taste of mankind, or some such fact, which may be the object of reasoning and inquiry" (XII (iii), p. 165).

Being a whole person Hume was concerned for moral practice as well as moral theory. He was attempting moral science as well as – though he did not make this distinction – moral philosophy. But he never made the mistake of thinking that the pursuit of understanding is inconsistent with the maintenance of lively practical engagements: "Man is a reasonable being; and as such, receives from science his proper food and nourishment . . . Man is a sociable, no less than a reasonable being . . . Man is also an active being . . ." (EHU I, p. 8).

In the discussion 'Of Morals' in Book III of the *Treatise*, the material "cast anew" in the second *Enquiry*, Hume is dealing with theoretical questions about present practice. This perhaps does something to explain those defections from a systematic ethical utilitarianism which Jeremy Bentham was to note, and regret. But even in such theoretical discussions Hume does not scruple to express his own outgoing, non-party, party commitment. Speaking of the principles from which the "moral sentiments" arise, he insists: "But these . . . we must remark, are social and universal; they form in a manner, the *party* of humankind against vice or disorder, its common enemy" (EPM IX (i), p. 275). He also concludes the *Treatise* with the claim that "the most abstract speculations concerning human nature, however cold and unentertaining, become subservient to *practical morality*; and may render this latter science more correct in its precepts, and more persuasive in its exhortations" (III (iii) 6, p. 621).

It has, since Samuel Johnson first said it, become notorious that "In lapidary inscriptions a man is not upon oath." Nevertheless it would appear that Adam Smith – who had known Hume ever since receiving, as an undergraduate at Balliol College, Oxford, a presentation copy of the *Treatise* – was not too generous in concluding his obituary tribute: "Upon the whole, I have always considered him, both in his lifetime and since his death, as approaching as nearly to the idea of a perfectly wise and virtuous man, as perhaps the nature of human frailty will permit" (DNR, pp. 247-8).

Hume was also prepared, when he saw the need, radically to rethink accepted moral ideas. Such rethinking was both a part and a consequence of his rejection of religion. (Or, perhaps we should say, his rejection, only but sufficiently, of any religion which should make any difference to human life?) In another letter to Hutcheson, responding to Hutcheson's comments on the manuscript of Book III of the *Treatise*, Hume confesses: "Upon the whole, I desire to take my Catalogue of Virtues from *Cicero's Offices*, not from the *Whole Duty of Man*. I had, indeed, the former book in my Eye in all my Reasonings" (Greig. 1932, I, p. 34). That "former book" is now known as the *de*

*Officiis* [*On Duties*], and is, as near as makes no matter, totally secular and this-worldly. Of the other it is sufficient to say that it has been ascribed to many authors, including no less than three archbishops.

There are many small indications of this realignment in the writings published during Hume's lifetime. But the most important product was the essay 'Of Suicide'. In this he argues that it is absurd to try to derive an absolute embargo on suicide from any idea of what is or is not natural, or from some difficult notion that such (or any) action would involve the illegitimate frustration of Omnipotence. He suggests that suicide can, on the contrary, sometimes be a right or even a duty. In this matter convictions reached in the study were certainly strengthened by personal experience. An incident in the campaign of 1746 led Hume to sigh: "But alas! we live not in Greek or Roman times" (Mossner, 1954, pp. 202-3). In all this Hume was obedient to his own most characteristic maxim: "Be a philosopher; but, amidst all your philosophy, be still a man" (EHU I, p. 9).

## 1 REASON AND PASSION, IS AND OUGHT

The third of the three sections relieving the general philosophical dreariness of Book II of the *Treatise* contains a sentence which has often been found scandalous: "Reason is, and ought only to be the slave of the passions, and can never pretend to any other office than to serve and obey them" (II (iii) 3, p. 415). This claim itself rarely is, yet ought always to be examined alongside another. That has, although only in relatively recent years, attracted an enormous amount of attention and dispute: "In every system of morality, which I have hitherto met with . . . the author proceeds for some time in the ordinary way of reasoning . . . when of a sudden I am surpriz'd to find, that instead of the usual copulations of propositions, *is*, and *is not*, I meet with no proposition that is not connected with an *ought*, or an *ought not*. This change is imperceptible; but is, however, of the last consequence. For as this *ought* or *ought not* expresses some new relation or affirmation, 'tis necessary that it shou'd be observ'd and explain'd; and at the same time that a reason should be given, for what seems altogether inconceivable, how this new relation can be a deduction from others which are entirely different from it" (ibid., III (i) 1,

p. 469): and, for controversy both about the interpretation of Hume and about the truth of what he was saying, compare Hudson, 1969).

The reason for examining these two claims in conjunction is that both have to be understood as expressions or consequences of Hume's fundamental insight about values. This crucial point has not been taken by those wanting to deny that the second states a simple but vastly important logical truth; the truth nowadays dubbed, eponymously, 'Hume's Law'. The least bad reason for that denial is the lack of any equally vivid and forceful successor passage in the second *Enquiry*. But then this is equally true of both. It is part of what makes that "a bland and insipid document"; rather than, as Hume himself asserted in his Autobiography, "of all my writings, historical, philosophical, or literary, incomparably the best". (How right he was to offer this as "my own opinion (who ought not judge on that subject)"!)

(i) "Reason is, and ought only to be the slave of the passions . . . " This utterance – as the parenthetical intrusion of the expression "and ought only to be" signals – should be construed as recommending that the key words 'reason' and 'passion' are in the present context to be read the one in a narrower and the other in a wider sense than is commonly the case. So interpreted, and discounting that parenthesis, the whole becomes a dramatized tautology. The prime object of the exercise is to enforce Hume's fundamental contention.

By employing the word 'reason' in the stricter sense thus recommended Hume becomes committed to many paradoxical and offensive conclusions: " 'Tis not contrary to reason to prefer the destruction of the whole world to the scratching of my finger. 'Tis not contrary to reason for me to chuse my total ruin, to prevent the least uneasiness of an *Indian* or person wholly unknown to me. 'Tis as little contrary to reason to prefer even my own acknowledg'd lesser good to my greater, and have a more ardent affection for the former than the latter" (THN II (iii) 3, p. 416). In this new, restricted sense "reason alone can never produce any action or give rise to volition . . ." (p. 414). Nor, by the same token, is it ever capable alone of inhibiting any sentiment or performance. For reason merely demonstrates abstract connections of ideas, or enables us to learn the brute relations of things. To know propositions is just to know propositions. It is not to prefer, to act, or even to refrain. The extended sense of 'passion' is just as paradoxical, but less offensive in its implications. For the word is here used to include every inclination which could conceivably constitute a motive for doing or not doing anything.

Hume's starting point is "the reality of moral distinctions". Any attempt to deny or to escape this – as we saw in section 2 of chapter 8 –he regards as perverse, fantastical, and disingenuous. So the question arises "whether they be derived from Reason, or from Sentiment . . ." (EPM I, pp. 169 and 170). As so often, he inclines more to what he takes to have been the general position of the ancients. In the first of the four appendices to the second *Enquiry* he allows that: "One principal foundation of moral praise being . . . the usefulness of any quality or action, it is evident that *reason* must enter for a considerable share in all decisions of this kind; since nothing but that faculty can instruct us in the tendency of qualities and actions, and point out their beneficial qualities to society and to their possessor" (p. 285). Yet this cannot be the whole story: "Utility is only a tendency to a certain end; and were the end totally indifferent to us we should feel the same indifference toward the means. It is requisite a *sentiment* should here display itself in order to give a preference to the useful over the pernicious tendencies" (p. 286).

In the second *Enquiry* it is identified as a general benevolence: "This sentiment can be no other than a feeling for the happiness of mankind, and a resentment of their misery . . ." (p. 286). The *Treatise* allowed only a restricted benevolence, extended through the mechanisms of sympathy. It asserts "that there is no such passion in human minds, as the love of mankind merely as such, independent of personal qualities, of services, or of relation to ourself" (III (ii) 1, p. 481). But such matters are unimportant compared with Hume's primary contention, that "after every circumstance, every relation is known, the understanding has no further room to operate, nor any object on which it could employ itself" (EPM App. I, p. 290). When all the work of description is done there is still the preference to be felt, the decision to be taken, the action to be performed.

In order to enforce Hume's fundamental contention about value in general, and moral value in particular, it was perhaps necessary to introduce, and to insist upon employing, this restricted sense of 'reason'. But its employment, if no other sense is admitted, does generate paradoxes. For in common and particularly in legal usage the reasonable man, besides being rational in a restricted Humian sense, also shows both a prudent regard for his own interests and some moderately benevolent concern for the welfare of others. These paradoxes have caused great distress. Kant, for instance, who presumably met our dramatized tautology quoted out of context in what Hume dismissed as "that bigotted silly fellow" Beattie's *Essay on the Nature and Immutability of Truth*, seems to have been so put out that he mistook the stating of a necessary truth for the setting of an insoluble problem: "But *how* pure reason can be practical in itself without further motives drawn from some other source . . . all human reason is totally incapable of explaining this, and all the effort and labour to seek such an explanation is wasted" (Kant, 1785, p. 129).

To relieve the distress of such critics Hume could, without in any way prejudicing his fundamental insight about the nature of value, admit second senses of 'reason' and 'reasonable'. This admission would call for the withdrawal of all such provocative statements as: "Actions may be laudable or blamable; but they cannot be reasonable or unreasonable." In the prime sense, in which "Reason is the discovery of truth and falshood" (THN III (i) 1, p. 458) a person's conduct could be described as reasonable only in virtue of their attention to relevant facts and consequences and their eschewing of plans of action bound to be self-frustrating. But in the second sense 'reasonable' would refer to a certain sober moderation in conduct; to a concern for impartiality, for consistency and for general rules.

To all those things Hume was himself – like the paradigmatically reasonable man of common speech – "mightily addicted". But such addictions must all be (dispositions to), in his own artificially extended sense, passions. So this is an admission which Hume could consistently make. In fact he does go at least some part of the way. For, in considering the importance of "general rules" in the direction of our moral sentiments, he refers to "what we formerly said concerning that reason, which is able to oppose our passion; and which we have found to be nothing but a general calm determination of the passions" (THN III (iii) 1, p. 583; and compare also II (iii) 3, p. 417, and II (iii) 8, pp. 437-8).

(ii) There is no question but that that oft-quoted epitome of Hume's views about the relations between reason and passion was a calculated provocation. The *Treatise*, after all, was and remains a young man's book – Hume's *Language, Truth and Logic*, so to speak (Ayer, 1946).

Certainly, as has just been shown, we cannot seize the full significance of that epitome unless we read it, as Kant could not and too many others do not, as summarizing much preceding argument. But Hume's Law in his actual formulation is not so much provocative as mischievously ironic. So we have in this case not only to be aware of the context but also to recognize the irony.

Here the expression is so far from being provocative that it is only in the last forty years that this passage has received the attention it merits. It is a remarkable fact, which deserves to be remarked more often, that *Principia Ethica*, in which G. E. Moore introduced the label 'Naturalistic Fallacy', makes no reference whatsoever to Hume. It is an even more remarkable fact that some professional philosophers, paid to know better, have missed the irony, and, pretending a superior and somewhat supercilious sophistication, have thought to refute Hume by pointing out that his sharp distinction between what is, and what ought to be, is not in fact always and everywhere made and observed (Hudson, 1969, pp. 120-34). But the truth, which ought to have been obvious, is that Hume's Law, like Hume's Fork, recommends a fundamental distinction as one which always can and should be made. These recommendations could not have the point and importance which they do have if the distinctions recommended were in fact universally accepted and remembered commonplaces.

The paragraph containing Hume's Law is at the end of a section which begins by emphasizing, in terms of Hume's own sharp separation of the scope of passion from that of reason, that morality falls within the former: "Morals excite passions, and produce or prevent actions. Reason of itself is utterly impotent in this particular" (THN III (i) 2, p. 457). He follows this up with a merry, if perhaps less than perfectly fair, refutation of a thesis attributed to the worthy William Wollaston; the thesis that the tendency to give rise to false belief is "the first spring or original source of all immorality" (p. 461).

Hume then considers the programme, projected by Locke and attempted by Spinoza, for a sort of moral geometry proceeding from self-evident and necessary premises. This he dismisses as chimerical, first, because there simply are no relations able to supply the premises required, and, second, because no such pure deductive system could be capable of bridging the gulf between abstract knowledge and practical obligation: "We cannot prove *a priori* that these relations, if they really existed and were perceived, would be universally forcible and obligatory" (p. 466). A similar situation obtains in the complementary case of matter of fact, which can be discovered by the understanding" (p. 468). For virtuousness and viciousness are not, nor yet are they directly deducible from, characteristics of situations in themselves. On the next page – the very page on which Hume's Law is formulated as an addendum "which may, perhaps, be found of some importance" – Hume draws the already quoted analogy between his own account of moral characteristics and the account of secondary qualities given in then recent physics.

When once that addendum is set, sympathetically, in the context of that to which it is added it becomes almost impossible to interpret it as saying anything but what it so clearly seems to say: namely, that there is a categorical difference between, on the one hand, pure calculating or detached describing and, on the other hand, engaged preferring or practical prescribing; and that we cannot, therefore, validly deduce conclusions about the latter from premises referring exclusively to the former.

It is when, but only when, all this is understood that the two sections of Part I of Book III fall into place as vital elements in the fulfilment of the project proclaimed in the Introduction to the *Treatise*. This, like that of Kant's first *Critique* (Kant, 1781, pp. 17-37), was a project for a kind of Copernican revolution in reverse. By this project human life on Earth is to become central again, especially in the concerns of the learned and on the map of knowledge; notwithstanding that our species is to be seen as just another species, a part albeit the most superior and important part of Nature. The final confirmation that Hume here is indeed picking out the Naturalistic Fallacy as indeed a fallacy comes when we notice that half the second of these two sections is devoted to considering whether prescriptive principles can be derived from descriptions of what is in some sense natural. Hume concludes, as he must: "'Tis impossible, therefore, that the character of natural and unnatural can ever, in any sense, mark the boundaries of vice and virtue" (p. 475).

## 2 VICE AND VIRTUE, PHILOSOPHY AND SCIENCE

There are, as has been remarked earlier, as between the *Treatise* and the second *Enquiry* some differences of substance in what Hume has to say 'Of Morals'. It is also worth noting what in the essay 'The Sceptic', first published in 1742, he presents as the one "certain and undoubted principle . . . which we learn from philosophy". It is a principle which he had himself in the *Treatise* devoted his best energies to establishing: "that there is nothing, in itself, valuable or despicable, beautiful or deformed; but that these attributes arise from the particular constitution and fabric of human sentiment and affection" (p. 162).

(i) One of these differences of substance is the allowing in the later treatment for a motive of generalized benevolence. Another lies in the accounts of virtue and vice. In the *Treatise* Hume sums up the results of examining a sample of what everyone must allow to be vicious action: "when you pronounce any action or character to be vicious, you mean nothing, but that from the constitution of your nature you have a feeling or sentiment of blame from the contemplation of it" (III (i) 1, p. 469). In the second *Enquiry* there is an appeal to the presumably impartial spectator: "The hypothesis which we embrace is plain . . . It defines virtue to be *whatever mental action or quality gives to a spectator the pleasing sentiment of approbation*; and vice the contrary" (App. I, p. 289).

Both these two passages have often been misconstrued as offering definitions of the words 'virtue' and 'vice'. These interpretations are quite mistaken, revealing a lamentable lack of understanding of and sympathy for Hume's intentions. Unlike Locke and Berkeley, he was not interested in questions which he saw as being merely verbal. This attitude is most strikingly manifested in the depreciation of his own "reconciling project"; it resolves a dispute which "has hitherto turned merely upon words" (EHU VIII (i), p. 81). So to construe either passage as embodying a premature contribution to the journal *Analysis* is just as wrong as are the parallel misinterpretations of what he does himself explicitly offer as "definitions" of 'cause'.

If the passages are taken as definitions, in the ordinary current sense, then the first is unbelievable and absurd. For any such definition is bound to imply that what are in truth head-on moral disagreements are really arguments completely at cross-purposes. To say that in denouncing something as wicked I am simply reporting my own reactions must make my relation to any opponent denying this both the same, and as ludicrous, as that of a person proposing to deny that someone else went somewhere yesterday by asserting that she herself did not. Had the Hume of the *Treatise* really held this position, as he was at one time

widely thought to have done (Broad, 1930, pp. 84-6; and compare
Harrison, 1976, pp. 62-3), then he would indeed have been a paradigm
case of an ethical subjectivist – in the narrowest sense; and a not very
great philosopher.

The second passage, similarly misconstrued, cannot be quite so
swiftly or so decisively refuted. But from its context it is even more
manifest: both what Hume actually is about; and that this certainly is
not attempting to describe established verbal usage. For, immediately
after the sentences quoted, Hume continues: "We then proceed to examine a plain matter of fact, to wit, what actions have this influence.
We consider all the circumstance in which these actions agree, and then
endeavour to extract some general observations with regard to these
sentiments. If you call this metaphysics, and find anything abstruse
here, you need only conclude that your turn of mind is not suited to the
moral sciences" (p. 289).

(ii) To analyse moral judgements as simply reporting the reactions of
those making those judgements is out of the question. But it is at least
not obviously wrong to suggest that at any rate some part of their
function is (not to report but rather) to express those reactions: "One
thing I might be doing in uttering 'X is good' is expressing a certain
feeling or sentiment I have towards X" (Stroud, 1977, p. 181). The
same writer continues, on the following page, "This 'emotivist' view
emphasizes the importance of feelings in moral 'judgements' . . . But
there is no evidence that Hume even considered such a theory."

That last assertion would make a formidable candidate were
anyone so perverse as to be awarding prizes for obtuse and preposterous commentary: it is as if some critic, after long study of the
novels of D. H. Lawrence, proposed to make much of that author's
reprehensible neglect of the sexual elements in human life. On the
very next page of the *Treatise*, following that to which this bizarre comment is supposed to relate, poor Hume, as if in a desperate effort to
forestall such crass misrepresentations, insists yet again: "Morality,
therefore, is more properly felt than judg'd of . . ." (III (i) 2, p. 470;
and compare Hudson, 1969, pp. 66-9).

What can sensibly be said is that he did not trouble to distinguish
the many particular possibilities falling under such general labels as
'emotivist' or 'subjectivist'. For the truth is "that Hume was not sufficiently interested in or worried about questions of meaning to

formulate clearly any such non-propositional view" (Mackie, 1980, p. 70).

Although Hume was certainly not a subjectivist, in the narrowest sense explained in the previous sub-section, he equally certainly was a subjectivist, in the comprehensive, catch-all sense indicated in the immediately preceding paragraph. He was indeed the intellectual forefather of all subsequent thinkers maintaining that, whatever they may be, what moral characteristics are not, is objective features of the various persons, institutions, actions and so on to which they are commonly attributed. That, after all, is a main element in his historic achievement.

(iii) It is perhaps worth adding a similar point about the senses in which Hume can and cannot be accounted a naturalist. In the factitious sense in which a naturalist becomes someone denying that the Naturalistic Fallacy really is a fallacy, Hume is the paradigm case of non-naturalism: "nothing can be more unphilosophical than those systems which assert that virtue is the same with what is natural, and vice with what is unnatural" (THN III (i) 2, p. 475).

But in another more general sense – like that in which Warburton, the friend of Pope and future Bishop of Gloucester, railed at the *Natural History of Religion* as designed "to establish naturalism, a species of atheism, instead of religion" (quoted in Greig, 1932, p. 248n) – Hume was unreservedly naturalistic. He believed firmly in an order of nature: it is a mark of the vulgar, not of the philosopher, to believe in the objectivity of chance. He showed no more patience with the old established division of history into sacred and profane than did Hippocrates towards the sacredness of 'the Sacred Disease' (epilepsy).

Again, Hume had no time for stories of miracles or claims to revelations; no room for any bifuraction into a natural and a supernatural order. The "will of the Supreme Being" rates merely perfunctory mention in the second *Enquiry* (App. I, p. 294). Both here and in the corresponding parts of the *Treatise* theological ideas are introduced only to provide examples of how principles intolerable in the solid affairs of common life may find sanctuary among such mental shades; and to reveal their distorting influence, intruding to warp "reasoning, and even language . . . from their natural course" (EHU App. IV, p. 322). The "true religion" advocated in the first *Enquiry* and the

*Dialogues* amounts to little more than a disguised rejecting of the whole dark business as a welter of troublesome superstitions.

There is a third, again rather artificial sense in which Hume might be called naturalistic. This would be derived from the fact that his thought provides so central a place for human nature. His analysis reduces experimental reasoning to customary brute behaviour, and the necessity of causes to the projection of felt human habits onto the world. Similarly, his argument here drives to the conclusion that while reason "discovers objects as they really stand in nature" human preference "has a productive faculty; and, gilding or staining all natural objects with the colours borrowed, raises, in a manner, a new creation" (App. I, p. 294). Morality is thus both man-centered and man-made.

(iv) Hume does not, however, mistake this to license or require the conclusions that its claims are either unimportant or arbitrary. (Furthermore, as we shall be seeing in chapter 10, he contends that, while certainly man-made rather than Divinely instituted, it is, like other major social institutions, not a product of individual or collective design but an unintended result of intending human action.) It is indeed neither unimportant nor arbitrary. Quite the contrary. Precisely because it is rooted in universal human desires, human needs, and human inclinations it becomes supremely important: "these principles . . . form, in a manner, the *party* of mankind . . ." (IX (i), p. 275). For the same reason, "Though the rules of justice be *artificial*, they are not *arbitrary*" (THN III (ii) 1, p. 484).

In another sense, that distinguished in the previous sub-section as the third in which Hume could truly be said to be a naturalist, they are supremely natural. In the essay entitled simply 'A Dialogue', an essay usually and rightly printed together with the second *Enquiry*, he considers the problem presented by the apparent variation of moral sentiments as between one culture or subculture and another. He insists that there is a basic uniformity beneath the superficial diversity: "the principles upon which men reason in morals are always the same; though the conclusions which they draw are often very different . . . there never was any quality recommended by anyone, as a virtue or a moral excellence, but on account of its being *useful* or *agreeable* to a man *himself* or to *others*" (pp. 335–6).

Rooting morality thus directly in human nature solves for Hume the problem of how it is possible for its being a duty to be a good, albeit perhaps defeasible, reason for doing something. (It was not open to him, as it might have been to a less secular moralist, to call on sanctions in a further life in order to provide us with a theoretically overwhelming interest in even the most uncongenial of our duties.) Hume seems sometimes to have been ambitious to do even more, to prove that moral obligation is really and unreservedly an indefeasible reason for action: "What theory of morals can ever serve any useful purpose unless it can show . . . that all the duties which it recommends are also the true interest of each individual? The peculiar advantage of the foregoing system seems to be that it furnishes proper mediums [i.e. middle terms – A.F.] for that purpose" (EPM IX (ii), p. 280; but compare pp. 283-4).

(v) There is in the final section of the second *Enquiry* one passage which seems never to have enjoyed a proper share of attention. It is, nevertheless, crisp, clear and richly suggestive: "When a man denominates another his *enemy*, his *rival*, his *antagonist*, his *adversary*, he is understood to speak the language of self-love, and to express sentiments, peculiar to himself, and arising from his particular circumstances and situation. But when he bestows on any man the epithets of *vicious* or *odious* or *depraved*, he then speaks another language, and expresses sentiments, in which he expects all his audience are to concur with him. He must here, therefore, depart from his private and particular situation, and must choose a point of view, common to him with others; he must move some universal principle of the human frame, and touch a string to which all mankind have an accord and symphony" (IX (i), p. 272).

Once this passage has been picked out, and pushed forward into isolated prominence, its significance becomes obvious. In three pellucid sentences Hume demonstrates that and why moral words simply cannot be defined in terms of the reactions, desires or interests of the individuals employing those words. His argument thus, in an entirely decisive way, rules right out: not only definitions which are in the narrowest sense subjectivist; but also anything on the lines of that proposed by Thrasymachus in Book I of *The Republic* (338C 1-3). It also indicates that no purely formal definition can suffice (Hare, 1952), So anyone daring to deny to Hume his proper place in the philosophical

Pantheon should be challenged to compare this argument with the feeble, often irrelevant and always peripheral script provided for Socrates by Plato at this key point (Flew, 1973).

# 10

# Evolutionary Emergence, or
# Contractual Creation?

In the *Treatise* Hume starts Part II of Book III by distinguishing artificial
from natural virtues: "there are some virtues, that produce pleasure
and approbation by means of an artifice or contrivance, which arises
from the circumstances and necessities of mankind" (III (ii) 1, p. 477).
But already by the end of the section he is conceding that the labels proposed are unsatisfactory: "Tho' the rules of justice be *artificial*, they are not
*arbitrary*. Nor is the expression improper to call them *Laws of Nature*; if
by natural we understand . . . what is inseparable from the species"
(p. 484). The second *Enquiry* never refers to artificial virtues, but introduces the expression 'social virtues'. Unfortunately this is there
applied, not only to 'justice and fidelity', but also to 'humanity and
benevolence' (App. III, pp. 304 and 303).

As Hume explains it, this distinction depends upon a puzzling yet
frequently reiterated claim: " 'Tis evident, that when we praise any
actions we regard only the motives that produced them, and consider
the actions as signs or indications of certain principles in the mind and
temper" (p. 477). But, we must object, this is not evident at all. If
anything here is evident, it is that motives are relevant to the assess-
ment: not of sorts of actions (type), the practical tendencies of which
are under review; but rather of an individual agent, who has performed
a particular action (token). Hume's reiteration of the present claim in
this Part II is the more puzzling and the more remarkable in that he is
going to say so much in the subsequent and final Part III about the
crucial importance for morality of the tendencies of actions (types).
Thus he says, rather as if he was wanting to emphasize his own inconsistency: "Tho' I am also of opinion, that reflexions on the tendencies
of actions have by far the greatest influence, and determine all the
great lines of our duty" (III (iii) 1, p. 590).

It was, after all, upon this final Part III of the *Treatise*, rather than the still more utilitarian second *Enquiry*, that Bentham made his famous comment: "That the foundations of all *virtue* are laid in *utility*, is there demonstrated, after a few exceptions made, with the strongest force of evidence: but I see not, any more than Helvetius saw, what need there was for the exceptions. For my own part, I well remember, no sooner had I read that part of the work which touches on this subject, than I felt as if the scales had fallen from my eyes. I then, for the first time, learnt that the cause of the people is the cause of virtue" (Bentham, 1776, I § 36, p. 50). In the later work Hume actually sets himself to prove "That public utility is the *sole* origin of justice . . ." (III (i), p. 183). It is in part this heavy and eventually exclusive emphasis upon utility, and in part his total rejection of any religious notions of this Earth as a vale of soul-making, which enables and requires Hume to admit into his gallery of the virtues many capacities and dispositions neither the outcomes of nor subject to the agent's choice and control.

The consensus of common sense is, surely, expressed in chapter II of *Utilitarianism*: "no known ethical standard decides an action to be good or bad because it is done by a good or a bad man, still less because done by an amiable, a brave, or a benevolent man, or the contrary. These considerations are relevant, not to the estimation of actions, but of persons . . . right action does not necessarily indicate a virtuous character, and . . . actions which are blamable often proceed from qualities entitled to praise" (Mill, 1861, p. 18). So whyever did it seem evident to Hume, however temporarily, that "when we praise any actions we regard only the motives that produced them"?

The least implausible answer so far suggested is that Hume somehow mistook this to be a consequence of his most fundamental contention, that value characteristics are a sort of secondary qualities. Thus in a section 'Of the origin of the natural virtues and vices', at the beginning of Part III, he says: "We have already observ'd, that moral distinctions depend entirely on certain peculiar sentiments of pain and pleasure, and that whatever mental quality in ourselves or others gives us a satisfaction . . . is of course virtuous; as every thing of this nature, that gives uneasiness, is vicious" (III (iii) 1, pp. 574-5). The route from "moral distinctions depend entirely on certain peculiar sentiments" to "when we praise any actions we regard only the motives that produced them" is, albeit precarious and unsound, short.

## 1 OF THE ORIGIN OF JUSTICE AND PROPERTY

In section 2 of this last part, under the present title, Hume sets himself "two questions, viz. *concerning the manner, in which the rules of justice are establish'd by the artifice of men*; and *concerning the reasons which determine us to attribute to the observance or neglect of these rules a moral beauty and deformity*" (p. 484).

(i) The first of these questions appears to be, and indeed is, historical or sociological; a reading which is confirmed when Hume goes on at once to say: "'Twas . . . a concern for our own, and the publick interest, which made us establish the laws of justice . . ." (p. 496); "And thus justice establishes itself by a kind of convention or agreement; that is, by a sense of interest, suppos'd to be common to all, and where every single act is perform'd in expectation that others are to perform the like" (p. 498). This obvious and correct reading is often overlooked. It is missed: partly because people who have pigeonholed Hume as a philosopher shut their eyes to the fact that he was so much else besides; and partly because he often speaks harshly of the notion of an historical social contract made to escape an historical state of nature.

Thus Hume says in this same section: ". . . philosophers may, if they please, extend their reasoning to the suppos'd *state of nature*; provided that they allow it to be a mere philosophical fiction, which never had, and never cou'd have any reality" (p. 493). And in section 7 he speaks in precisely parallel terms about the legend of an historical social contract (pp. 541-2).

These passages may well remind us of the *Dissertation on the Origin and Foundation of Inequality*: "Let us begin then by laying facts aside, as they do not affect the question. The investigations we may enter into, in treating this subject, must not be considered as historical truths, but only as mere conditional and hypothetical reasonings . . ." (Rousseau, 1762, p. 161). But the reason why Hume rejects the notions of a pre-social state of nature and of an original social contract is: not at all that he is "laying facts aside, as they do not affect the question"; but, on the contrary, that such "mere philosophical fiction . . . never had, and never cou'd have any reality". What Hume is interested in just is the origin and nature of fundamental social institutions. These, he argues, neither did nor could have emerged through a social contract from a pre-social state of nature; if only because promising itself presupposes the essentially social institution of language. In reading the *Treatise* we should never forget that we are reading the prolegomena to the entire Edinburgh Enlightment; a broad cultural movement of which Hume was himself later to become the acknowledged doyen.

Hume's own solution to this problem of origins is subtle, hard-headed, and profound; notwithstanding that some of the terms in which he states that solution must, unfortunately, suggest the sociologically unsophisticated crudities which he himself is striving to reject. Where his less enlightened opponents tell tales referring back to deliberate foresight and contractual agreement, Hume argues that the fundamental social institutions could not have originated from this sort of planning. What is possible is that recognitions of common interest will lead to the regulation of conduct in ways which are not, and in this case could not be, derived from prior contracts: "Two men, who pull the oars of a boat, do it by an agreement or convention, tho' they have never given promises to each other. Nor is the rule concerning the stability of possession the less deriv'd from human conventions, that it arises gradually, and acquires force by a slow progression . . . In like manner are languages gradually establish'd by human conventions without any promise. In like manner do gold and silver become the common measures of exchange . . ." (p. 490).

Hume's approach to the origin of social institutions is thus evolutionary as opposed to creationist; and a main insight of any such sophisticated understanding is that social institutions, which are of course purely human productions, may have functions and consequences which are not the fulfilments of anyone's intentions. In section 6, 'Some farther reflexions concerning justice and injustice' he observes: " 'Tis self-love which is their real origin; and as the self-love of one person is naturally contrary to that of another, these several interested passions are oblig'd to adjust themselves after such a manner as to concur in some system of conduct and behaviour. This system, therefore, comprehending the interest of each individual, is of course advantageous to the public; tho' it be not intended for that purpose by the inventors" (p. 529).

It is, therefore, not without reason that Hume in the footnote to his Introduction lists Dr Mandeville among his predecessors. For what is this basic insight that men "stumble upon establishments, which are indeed the result of human action, but not the execution of any human design" (Ferguson, 1767, p. 122), if it is not Mandeville's notorious "Private Vices, Publick Benefits", reapplied without any distracting desire to scandalize? Hume's younger friend Adam Smith was working within a tradition of emerging sociological sophistication when he wrote of the person deciding where to invest or to disinvest (not the anonymous taxpayer's but) his own personal capital: "He generally, indeed, neither intends to promote the publick interest, nor knows how much he is promoting it . . . he intends only his own security, and he is in this, as in many other cases, led by an invisible hand to promote an end which was no part of his intentions." To which, as if foreseeing our ever-lengthening list of ruinous, wealth-wasting decisions made ('not for private profit but in the public interest') by bureaucrats and politicians, an insightful author adds: "Not is it always the worse for the society that it was no part of it. By pursuing his own interest he frequently promotes that of the society more efficiently than when he really intends to promote it" (Smith, 1776, IV (ii), p. 456).

This association of Hume with Adam Smith, Adam Ferguson and other Scottish founding fathers of social science suggests two comments. First, it is diametrically wrong to interpret this invisible hand as that of a beneficent Providence, producing only consequences guaranteed to be good. Smith himself made much of a similar social mechanism producing unintended consequences many of which are much less happy. So much so that his denunciation of evils arising from the division of labour – what Hume, learning from Mandeville, had earlier picked out as "the partition of employments" (THN III (ii) 2, p. 485) – is quoted with approval in *Capital* (Marx, 1867, I, p. 362). The truth is that Smith's invisible hand is no more the hand of a beneficent Providence than Darwin's natural selection is God's conscious choice.

The second comment appropriate to the present context is that the work of Hume and of other leading figures of the Edinburgh Enlightenment prepared the way for Darwin, and was in fact used by him (Flew, 1984, III 2). Whereas they had shown that various social institutions which looked to be products of deliberate design might or even must have evolved rather than been consciously created, Darwin was to go on to apply the same ideas to all species of organisms. Hume in particular often appears to be groping after the possibility of grounding his whole philosophy upon an account of man's place in Nature which was not to become fully available until the subsequent century (Ruse, 1986). Thus, in the first *Enquiry*, commenting on the place of custom or habit in argument from experience, Hume writes: "As nature has taught us the use of our limbs . . . so has she implanted in us an instinct, which carries forward the thought in a correspondent course to that which she has established among external objects . . ." (V (ii), p. 55). The same idea of adaptation, as well as a suggestion of natural selection, is seen in the *Dialogues*: "It is in vain, therefore, to insist upon the uses of the parts in animals or vegetables, and their curious adjustment to each other. I would fain know how an animal could subsist, unless its parts were so adjusted" (VIII, p. 185; and compare Gaskin, 1978, pp. 36-9).

## 2 OF THE RULES, WHICH DETERMINE PROPERTY

To the first of the two questions set at the beginning of section 2 in the penultimate part of the *Treatise* Hume answers: that "justice establishes itself by a kind of convention or agreement; that is, by a sense of interest, suppos'd to be common to all, and where every single act is perform'd in expectation that others are to perform the like" (p. 484).

The second is answered most fully in section 6. This utilitarian answer is further supported by other utilitarian arguments both in the final part of the *Treatise* and elsewhere. It is so important to distinguish both the different questions and the different answers that this answer had better be quoted again. The real origin of the rules of justice is, Hume maintains, self-love. That is why it is not a natural but an artificial virtue: "as the self-love of one person is naturally contrary to that of another, these several interested persons are oblig'd to adjust themselves after such a manner as to concur in some system of conduct and behaviour. This system, therefore, comprehending the interest of each individual, is of course advantageous to the public; tho' it be not intended for that purpose by the inventors."

The need to have any rules at all, as opposed to some one particular set, arises from two features of human condition: "*the selfishness and confin'd generosity of men, along with the scanty provision nature has made for his wants*" (III (ii) 2, p. 495). Suppose that everything were as inexhaustibly available to all comers as fresh air in the Rockies, or suppose that everyone loved their neighbours as themselves; then – Hume

says – there would be no need for any institution drawing lines between mine and his and yours. But in fact, as things actually are, we
all have an overriding interest in the preservation of this institution;
"since, without justice, society must immediately dissolve, and
everyone must fall into that savage and solitary condition, which is infinitely worse than the worst situation that can possibly be suppos'd in
society" (p. 497). Especially in what Wittgenstein so loved to call "the
darkness of these times", before proceeding to Hume's third question, two things need to be emphasized. The first is that we should
construe any talk of Hume's views about the distribution of property
in a strictly inactive sense of 'distribution'. The second is that
Hume's almost Hobbist appreciation of the horrors of a state of
nature provides his reason for recommending us all to accept
whatever are the established and viable principles of distribution,
however far these may defect from our individual ideals.

It is also worth noting here that Hume provides in the Third
Appendix to the second *Enquiry* an early source for a point crucial to
our entire contemporary debate about rule as against act
utilitarianism: "The result of the individual acts is . . ., in many instances, directly opposite to that of the whole system of actions; and
the former may be extremely hurtful, while the latter is, to the highest
degree, advantageous" (p. 304). In the fourth Appendix – contrary
to what had seemed so evident to the author of the *Treatise* – Hume insists that emphasis on the motives and actual intentions of agents is a
theological corruption of sound natural morals: "Philosophers, or
rather divines under that disguise, treating all morals on a like footing
with civil laws . . . were necessarily led to render this circumstance, of
*voluntary* or *involuntary*, the foundation of their whole theory" (p. 322).

Hume's third question seeks the substantial content of these rules.
Here the first puzzle is why, having previously spoken of justice and
property, he now speaks only 'Of the rules, which determine property'. The nearest he comes to discussing criminal justice, and fairness
in the enforcement of law and order generally, is in passing
references, particularly and most crucially in section 7 'Of the origin
of government', to the menace of "that wretched and savage condition, which is commonly represented as the *state of nature*" (p. 534).
He may have thought, with reason, that he had a greater contribution
to make concerning the determination of property rights. Or he may
have been employing, more or less deliberately, a more comprehen-

sive conception of property: "From all which it is evident, that though the things of Nature are given in common, yet Man (by being Master of himself, and *Proprietor of his own Person*, and the Actions or *Labour* of it) had still in himself *the great Foundation of Property* . . ." (Locke, 1690b, p. 316).

The second occasion for comment is that Hume has taken to heart the warning given by Plato's Socrates at the end of Book I of *The Republic* (354C 1-5). For although Hume has little patience with questions seen as merely verbal he does not make the mistake of thinking that he can answer important substantive questions about justice without knowing what justice is (Flew, 1981, ch. III 2; and contrast Rawls, 1971, p. 579). He remembers enough from the days when he was supposedly, according to the Autobiography, not "poring over Voet and Vinnius", as he was supposed to be, to be able and willing to quote "The vulgar definition of justice . . . *a constant and perpetual will of giving everyone his due*" (THN III (ii) 5, p. 526). This is a word for word translation of a formulation found in Book I of the *Institutes* of Justinian. Indeed until John Rawls's *A Theory of Justice* burst upon the scene every treatise purporting to deal with this subject must have developed some variation upon that same theme – allowing to everyone their several, and often presumably very different, deserts and entitlements.

Hume's own answer to the question of what ought to determine property rights is equally traditional. It is expressed as consisting in "the three fundamental laws of nature, *that of the stability of possession, of its transference by consent*, and *of the performance of promises*" (THN III (ii) 6, p. 526). Whereas Locke starts from a hypothetical or fictitious past situation in which nothing is owned (save persons, their parts and their personal potentialities), and asks how legitimate titles to separate goods and chattels might have been originally acquired, Hume begins from the position in which we and he in fact find ourselves, and considers how property ought and ought not to be obtained or retained in that contemporary context. The second and third of his three "laws of nature" embrace all the cases confronted in the normal course of things by those not born into a state of nature. We most of us acquire whatever property and income we do from time to time acquire: either thanks to gifts inter vivos or to legacies ("transference by consent"); or else through some kind of contractual exchange ("the performance of promises").

The last point will bear a good bit of pondering. It would seem never to have been taken either by Rawls himself or by most of those who have so eagerly accepted his approach, if not the whole of his detailed working out of that approach. For his hypothetical contracting parties, without either question or hesitation, begin by taking it for granted that all goods either already available or in the future to be produced within their to them unknown state frontiers are available for distribution or redistribution at their own absolute discretion, unburdened by any legitimate prior claims, whether internal or external. Such goods even include, presumably, services which are individual human actions (Flew, 1981, ch. III-IV).

This may, arguably, be the conclusion which we ought to reach in the end. Yet the always defeasible presumptions from which we should at least begin are, surely, those indicated by Hume? Whoever is in fact in possession must be presumed to be the true owner; while, presumably, any transfers of holdings must be by consent, whether in the performance of promises or otherwise.

The case which Hume offers for accepting his three principles in property distribution is unequivocally utilitarian: " 'Tis on the strict observance of those three laws, that the peace and security of human society entirely depend; nor is there any possibility of establishing a good correspondence among men, where these are neglected. Society is absolutely necessary for the well-being of men; and these are as necessary to the support of society" (THN III (ii) 6, p. 526).

Rawls, by contrast, sees "the first principle of justice" as "one requiring an equal distribution" (p. 150). He derives it as the putative presupposition of a hypothetical social contract made behind a "Veil of Ignorance" (pp. 136-42). This veil conceals from the participants all particulars of their actual natures and situations. These, by a bizarre Rawlsian fiat, are dismissed as "arbitrary from a moral point of view" (p. 15). Notice too that this perfect egalitarian principle is a substantive affirmation of what is presumably supposed to become an universal human right. It should not be confused with a merely methodological insistence that any deviation has to be warranted by some kind of sufficient reason.

Rawls immediately supplements, rather than qualifies, his radically egalitarian ideal with one important concession: "If there are inequalities in the basic structure that work to make everyone better off in comparison with the benchmark of initial equality, why not permit them?" (p. 151). It is, therefore, both apt and illuminating to regard any inequalities which Rawls will eventually be prepared to tolerate as the outcomes of hypothetical productivity bargains: those who are to be relatively less well off agree to trade, in return for some advance beyond the (surely miserable) absolute level at which all would otherwise have been equal, some part of a most fundamental, putative human right – the surly and envious Rawlsian right not to be excelled!

It is surely, significant that this egalitariansim of outcome (Flew, 1981, ch. II 5), which apparently presents itself both to Rawls and to many others today as the obvious first principle of justice, does not here even occur to Hume as an alternative demanding attention. The only alternative which Hume mentions in the *Treatise*, only to dismiss, is precisely not in any understanding egalitarian. It is that justice requires that everyone should have whatever is appropriate to their particular and different natures and circumstances: " 'Twere better, no doubt, that every one were possess'd of what is most suitable to him, and proper for his use: But besides, that this relation may be common to several at once, 'tis liable to so many controversies, and men are so partial and passionate in judging of these controversies, that such a loose and uncertain rule wou'd be absolutely incompatible with the peace of human society. The convention concerning the stability of possession is enter'd into, in order to cut off all the occasions of discord and contention . . . Justice, in her decisions, never regards the fitness or unfitness of objects to particular persons, but conducts herself by more extensive views" (III (ii) 3, p. 502).

When later, in Section III (ii) of the second *Enquiry*, Hume does entertain the notion of "an equal distribution of property" it is to dismiss this as impracticable, and in any case pernicious: "Render possessions ever so equal, men's different degrees of art, care, and industry will immediately break that equality. Of if you check these virtues, you reduce society to the most extreme indigence; and instead of preventing want and beggary in a few, render it unavoidable to the whole community. The most rigorous inquisition too is requisite to watch over inequality on its first appearance; and the most severe jurisdiction, to punish and redress it" (p. 194).

We may note, perhaps in our time somewhat ruefully, that Hume was optimist enough to believe that any authority so intrusive and inquisitorial as this – which "must soon degenerate into tyranny and be exerted with great partialities" – would be inherently precarious and self destructive. There is not, however, room here for any thorough investigation of such practical matters. But, in a period when it is hard to get a sympathetic hearing in academic circles for arguments against actively Procrustean redistribution between individuals, one way of eroding "that implicit faith and security, which is the bane of all reasoning and free enquiry" may be to set the issues in an international context.

So consider, first, the case of the African frontiers. The present land boundaries of most of the new African states were originally drawn before any of these states had even been thought of, and before any of their inhabitants had aspired to build a future nation. They were drawn always by Europeans and often across territories which, though already inhabited, had not yet been explored by outsiders. In consequence they are frequently arbitrary; and incongruous with geographical, tribal or economic realities. Nevertheless the Organization for African Unity is for once unanimous, and here voices what is clearly a sensible continental consensus, in insisting on "the stability of possession"; the former colonial and present sovereign state frontiers can be altered only, if at all, "by consent". The justification for living with the anomalies – and it is, surely, a very good if not necessarily and always an indefeasibly good reason – is "in order to cut off . . . occasions of discord and contention."

Notice next that Rawls, like so many others, applies his fundamentally egalitarian conceptions only to a single society; although without ever offering us any reason for holding that state frontiers properly either invalidate or weaken "the first principle of justice . . . requiring an equal distribution". Yet that principle implies, not only a right not to be excelled, but also a duty not oneself to excel. It is – notoriously, albeit very understandably – more difficult to find sincere and consistent spokesmen for the second than for the first of these complementary implications; and this embarrassment is displayed most vividly by extreme international comparisons. Consider, for example, electorally attractive policies for, in the gleefully sadistic words of one recent British Chancellor, "making the rich howl in anguish". On what grounds of egalitarian principle can enthusiasts for this programme justify the redistribution of the proceeds of thus "soaking the rich": not to the poorest of the poor in – say – Dahomey or Bangladesh; but to the British not so rich?

It is hard to excogitate any answer which does not refer to British rights to capital stocks built up by previous British generations; and parallel responses to similar challenges are in fact regularly given by spokesmen for the various fully socialist countries of the Soviet bloc. But to make any appeal of this sort is to abandon the Rawls "first principle of justice . . . equal distribution", in favour of a Humian foundation in the "the stability of possession". The enormous difference between any such new move and that old original lies in the dimension of collectivism. For Hume legitimate owners are, typically, flesh and blood individuals. For the others all property, or at any rate most, is properly and in the first instance vested in a collectivity, the people, or society; and hence, in practice, in the state.

## 3 PERSONAL PROMISES AND SOCIAL CONTRACTS

In the *Treatise* the four sections on justice and property are followed by section 5 'Of the obligation of promises'. Although, philosophically, this is one of the most interesting and valuable in the whole book it is only recently that it seems to have achieved due recognition. This material was never "cast anew" by Hume either in the second *Enquiry* or elsewhere. All that he did there was ridicule the suggestion "that justice arises from Human Conventions and proceeds from the voluntary choice, consent or combination of mankind." For "If by *convention* is here meant a *promise* (which is the most usual sense of the word) nothing can be more absurd than this position. The observance of promises is one of the most considerable parts of justice, and we are not surely bound to keep our word because we have given our word to keep it" (App. III, p. 306).

(i) In the *Treatise* Hume sets himself to prove two propositions. In one the key word 'convention' is employed in a very necessary sense, but a sense quite other than what, on his own later account, "is most usual". He is speaking of "the rule of morality, which enjoins the performance of promises", and the two propositions are: *"that a promise wou'd not be intelligible, before human conventions had establish'd it;* and *that even if it were intelligible, it wou'd not be attended with any obligation"* (III (ii) 5, p. 516).

In Humian terms the fulfilment of promises is, of course, an artificial rather than a natural virtue. So his discussion is throughout conducted upon the false assumption first stated in introducing that distinction: " 'Tis evident, that when we praise any actions, we regard only the motives that produced them, and consider the actions as signs or indications of certain principles in the mind or temper" (III (ii) 1, p. 477). The unfortunate consequence is that Hume becomes committed to seeking some crucial "act of the mind", conceived in Cartesian terms as a purely mental action without any essential involvement of the corporeal. Although he quickly concludes that there is no such thing, and that even if there were it could not give rise to an obligation, he still believes that "we *feign* a new act of the mind, which we call willing an obligation; and on this we suppose the morality to depend" (p. 523; and compare Mackie, 1980, pp. 102-3).

This Cartesian relic, however, is eminently dispensable. The main and, surely, correct contention here is that the obligation of promises is created not by some internal and secret commitment but by the entirely public and physical action of giving our word. Purely private reservations may make the promise dishonest, but do not extinguish the obligation. It is, therefore, noteworthy that J. L. Austin made no mention of Hume either in his first discussion of promising and performative utterance generally, in the 1946 symposium on 'Other Minds', or in his most extended treatment, in the 1955 William James lectures on *How to do Things with Words* (1961, pp. 44-84; and 1962b, especially pp. 9-10). But compare some earlier, desperately perplexed remarks by a predecessor as White's Professor of Moral Philosophy (Prichard, 1949, pp. 169-79).

Having to his own satisfaction successfully completed his unsuccessful search for the supposedly crucial "act of the mind", Hume goes on to argue the need for the artificial social institution of promising. Huge as is the benefit of having established the equally artificial "three fundamental laws of nature" determining the just distribution of property, until that institution too is available innumerable exchanges which would advantage both parties cannot in practice be effected. I would, for instance, be delighted to help you get in your harvest today, if only I could be sure that in return you would help me with mine tomorrow. So, happily, "there is a *certain form of words* invented"; or, rather, an institutional solution is evolved.

"This form of words constitutes what we call a *promise*, which is the sanction of the interested commerce of mankind. When a man says he *promises any thing*, he in effect expresses a resolution of performing it; and along with that, by making use of this *form of words*, subjects himself to the penalty of never being trusted again in case of failure." Promises are thus "the conventions of men, which create a new motive, when experience has taught us, that human affairs wou'd be conducted much more for mutual advantage, were there certain *symbols* or *signs* instituted . . . After these signs are instituted, whoever uses them is immediately bound by his interest to execute his engagements, and must never expect to be trusted any more, if he refuse to perform what he promis'd" (p. 522).

Having thus discovered one particular kind of case in which uttering a sentence is actually performing some action, or bringing about some effect, rather than merely describing or reporting what is supposed to be the case already, Hume goes on to suggest that there are also other kinds. But he prefers not to present innocuous and obvious candidates, such as giving a name to a ship or casting a verbal vote. His alternative suggestions are more mischievous: "transubstantiation, or *holy orders*, where a certain form of words, along with a certain intention, changes entirely the nature of an external object, and even of a human creature" (p. 524).

What he has is mind is the claim that the uttering of certain ritual words in ceremonials conducted by duly qualified persons produces essential, albeit practically undetectable, transformations. In the one case the words of the priest are supposed to replace the substance (but not the appearances) of bread and wine by the substance (but not the appearances) of flesh and blood. In the other the words of the bishop are alleged to imprint an "*indelible character*" upon the recipient.

The moral which Hume delights to draw is that those religious institutions, and this of promising, are totally different, both in their origins and in their human importance. That, he urges, shines out, since "Theologians . . . have commonly determin'd, that the intention of the priest makes the sacrament, and that when he secretly withdraws his intention, he . . . destroys the baptism, or communion, or holy orders." Such esoteric frivolity, Hume happily allows, is, in religion, all very well. But in the serious business of everyday life it will not do. Here "the . . . consequence . . . of a similar doctrine, with regard to promises, have prevented that doctrine from establishing itself." The discussion has a well-contented conclusion: "Men are always more concern'd about the present life than the future; and are apt to think the smallest evil, which regards the former, more important than the greatest, which regards the latter" (p. 525).

(ii) We have noticed already that Hume rejects most categorically any idea that governments in fact originated, or continue to derive their authority, from actual social contracts, by which the contracting parties released themselves from a previous state of nature. But he was equally concerned to emphasize that the principle, which many thought to establish by this roundabout route, "is perfectly just and reasonable" (THN III (ii) 9, p. 549). This same principle, "that our submission to government admits of exceptions, and that an egregious tyranny in the rulers is sufficient to free the subjects from all ties of allegiance" (p. 549), Hume himself proposed to establish in a more direct and relevant way. After all, why should anyone today consider themselves bound by an unrecorded contract made by their remotest ancestors?

Fully to appreciate what is going on here we need to bring into our reckoning several of Hume's later political essays, especially 'Of the Parties of Great Britain' and 'Of the Original Contract'. For this theoretical justification for the practical principle was a doctrine of the Whigs. So much so that it was embodied in the crucial decisions of the House of Commons on 28 and 29 January 1689; the operative resolutions which legitimized the Glorious Revolution. One of these ran: "Resolved that King James II, having endeavoured to subvert the constitution of his kingdom by breaking the original contract between King and Parliament, and by the advice of Jesuits and other wicked persons having violated the fundamental laws; and having withdrawn himself out of his kingdom, has abdicated the government; and the throne is thereby vacant."

Hume, therefore, proceeds: "I shall not take such a compass, in establishing our political duties, as to assert that men perceive the advantages of government," and, so perceiving, establish it by consenting to a social contract. "I perceive, that a promise itself arises entirely from human conventions, and is invented with a view to a certain interest. I seek, therefore, some such interest more immediately connected with government and which may be at once the original motive to its institution, and the source of our obedience to it . . . As interest, therefore, is the immediate sanction of government the one can have no longer being than the other; and whenever the civil magistrate carries his oppression so far as to render his authority perfectly intolerable, we are no longer bound to submit to it" (THN III (ii) 9, pp. 550-1).

Conventions here, as the whole context makes plain, are patterns of habitual behaviour, of a kind arising prior to the possibility of either promising or any other essentially linguistic performance. The subsistence of such conventions is indeed "that something implied in the existence of agreements which looks very much like an agreement and yet, strictly speaking, cannot be an agreement" (Prichard, 1949, p. 179). The word 'invention' here also needs to be glossed. It has to be read as implying, as its etymology suggests, more an establishment stumbled upon (Ferguson, 1767, pp. 122-3), than one erected with calculating and competent intention.

It is the more necessary to emphasize all these points since in the very next section Hume at least appears to contradict himself: "the authority of the magistrate does *at first* stand on the foundation of a promise of the subjects, by which they bind themselves to obedience; as in every other contract or engagement" (p. 554). This has misled one of the soundest of contemporary Hume scholars to assert, without qualification, that Hume "accepts, from the Social Contract theorists, the theory that in the first instance governments must come into existence through the subjects making an explicit promise to obey a magistrate" (Penelhum, 1975, p. 159).

A resolution of this apparent contradiction can, however, be discovered in the essay 'Of the Original Contract'. For there Hume allows that he would concede "the *original contract*", but only in a much extended sense: "No contract or agreement, it is evident, was expressly formed for general submission; an idea far beyond the comprehension of savages: Each exertion of authority in the chieftan must have been particular, and called forth by the present exigencies of the case: The sensible utility, resulting from his interposition, made these exertions become daily more frequent; and their frequency gradually produced an habitual, and, if you please to call it so, voluntary . . . acquiescence in the people" (pp. 468-9; and compare Brownsey, 1978).

## 4 HUME'S CONSERVATISM

It is only rather recently that it has begun to be argued that Hume, rather than Burke, should be seen as the first forefather of the modern conservative intellectual tradition. The main reason for this delay must have been Hume's notoriety as an infidel: "the Church is my aversion" (Mossner, 1954, p. 234). For it is, again, only rather recently that the mainstream churches in the USA, Britain, and several other countries have taken to issuing statements supporting distinctively socialist political and social causes (Anderson, 1984). For instance: at the time of writing, the British Council of Churches is running on the London Underground a poster campaign the sole message of which is a call to pray for the peaceful and unresisted maintenance of a Marxist–Leninist regime in Nicaragua; an expensive campaign apparently financed by a registered charity calling itself Christian Aid. Similar spiritual support is very conspicuously not offered to the Christian Democrat regime in neighbouring San Salvador, in its resistance to a Marxist–Leninist insurgency.

But there have been other reasons for the delay in recognizing this truth about Hume. One is the failure to appreciate how much of classical liberalism there is in that conservative tradition, and how little in the modern Liberal Party. Adam Smith himself once remarked that "Burke is the only man I ever knew who thinks on economic subjects exactly as I do, without any previous communications between us" (Rae, 1895, pp. 387–8); while one count revealed that four-fifths of the votes in the last parliament found Liberal members in the same lobby as Labour. Hume himself lived long enough to study his presentation copy of *The Wealth of Nations*, and to express the hope that he and his friend Smith might deal together with several minor points of disagreement "fit only to be discussed in Conversation" (Greig, 1932, II, p. 312). On all the main issues they were agreed. In his essay 'Of the Jealousy of Trade', for instance, Hume demolishes the mean misconception that commercial exchange must be a zero-sum operation. "In opposition to this narrow and malignant opinion," he concludes: "not only as a man, but as a BRITISH subject, I pray for the flourishing commerce of GERMANY, SPAIN, ITALY, and even FRANCE itself" (pp. 328 and 331; and compare Flew, 1981, ch. V).

Another and more relevant reason for the delay is that much of the evidence is in either the *Essays* or the *History* rather than the four chief philosophical works (Livingston, 1984, Ch. 10-12). The commitment to the substantive principles of the Glorious Revolution, though not to its traditional justification, was as strong in Hume as in Burke. It was this commitment which led both men to sympathize with what was the thoroughly Whiggish American Revolution. In his essay 'Of the Protestant Succession' Hume speaks of the years since the first of these events with a rare lack of reserve: "So long and so glorious a period no nation almost can boast of: Nor is there another instance in the whole history of mankind, that so many millions of people have, during such a space of time, been held together, in a manner so free, so rational, and so suited to the dignity of human nature" (p. 508).

Again, in the *History* Hume saw many of the opponents of Charles I as Burke was to see the Jacobins. Both groups, the one in the name of revelation and the other of reason, were resolved to make all things new, living each day as if their first. When Louis XVI, to whom at the age of ten Hume had been presented at court, and who both earlier and later studied the *History* with care, learned that the Convention had voted the death sentence, he told his valet to fetch the volume dealing with the execution of Charles I (Livingston, 1984, p. 317). In the essay 'Of the Original Contract' Hume makes very clear his rejection of such unconservative and, in the Hayekian sense, rationalist revolution: "Did one generation go off the stage at once, as is the case with silkworms and butterflies, the new race . . . might establish their own form of civil polity, without any regard to the laws or precedents, which prevailed among their ancestors . . . Some innovations must necessarily have place in every human institution . . . but violent innovations no individual is entitled to make; they are even dangerous to be attempted by the legislature . . ." (pp. 476-7; and compare Hayek, 1967, ch. 5).

But, although the political applications are mainly in the *Essays* and the *History*, the principles themselves are all in the more narrowly philosophical works, beginning with the *Treatise*. Always Hume insists: both that the scope and potentialities of human reason are limited; and that we are, above all, creatures of habit. If we cannot even know that there are mind-independent realities in an External World, how absurd it is to think that we could form and execute some scheme of wholesale utopian social engineering having all but only the benign consequences allegedly intended. As creatures of habit we must be forever liable to relapse into our former ways, while both resenting and struggling against the disappointment of long-cherished expectations. The burden of proof, therefore, must rest always on the would-be innovator.

At a somewhat more profound level there is a similarly conservative moral to be drawn from Hume's insights into the origin of fundamental social institutions. For if these were not designed and first constructed by culture heroes – or even by heroic culture committees – but instead evolved as the unplanned and uncoordinated products of intended and unintended human interactions; then it is no longer sensible to assume that we, standing on their shoulders, can straightway and easily design and erect superior replacements. If we are even to make less wholesale improvements, which really will be improvements, then we shall need first thoroughly to study the present workings of whatever existing institutions we do sincerely wish to improve.

It is perhaps apt to end this chapter, and the whole book, with an illustration of prudent philosophical conservatism leading to conservatism in philosophy. Hume himself despised issues which he saw as merely verbal, though he was seized of two crucial points: both that the natural languages are the most important and the most complex of all human creations; and that the learning and use of these is a matter of acquiring and exercising habits (THN I (i) 7, p. 23). So consider a modern approach to questions of linguistic reform; not Hume's, nevertheless – whatever the author's own intentions – entirely Humian. In his overture to virtuoso revelations of the rarely noticed richness of our ordinary, non-technical vocabulary of extenuation and excuse, this writer maintains: "our common stock of words embodies all the distinctions men have found worth drawing, and the connexions they have found worth marking, in the lifetimes of many generations: these surely are likely to be more numerous, more sound, since they have stood up to the long test of the survival of the fittest, and more subtle, at least in all ordinary and reasonably practical matters, than any you or I are likely to think up in our arm-chairs of an afternoon –the most favoured alternative method" (Austin, 1961, p. 130).

In the seventies this passage became a favourite whipping boy for contributors to widely distributed collections of Radical essays. Usually in quoting they omitted both the reference to "the survival of the fittest" and the qualification "at least in all ordinary and reasonably practical matters". Always they added some contemptuous comment: "To others of us it is at least equally reasonable to think that new and unfamiliar experiences or ways of seeing the world and human nature may require the formulation of new concepts and new theories, rather than efforts to cram them into old and established categories" (Arblaster, 1970, pp. 36-7; and compare Flew, 1976b, ch. 8).

These performances should remind us that wanton misrepresentation of an opponent always is, and is always to be construed as, a confession of the misrepresenter's inability to refute that opponent in fair and open intellectual combat. For, three pages later, the author thus criticized glosses those carefully omitted clauses: "If a distinction works well for practical purposes in ordinary life (no mean feat, for ordinary life is full of hard cases), then there is sure to be something in it, it will not mark nothing: yet this is likely enough not to be the best way of arranging things if our interests are more extensive and intellectual than ordinary. And again, that experience has been derived only from the sources available to ordinary men throughout most of civilized history: it has not been fed from the resources of the microscope and its successors. Certainly then, ordinary language is *not* the last word: in principle it can everywhere be supplemented and improved upon and superseded. Only remember, it *is* the *first* word" (Austin, 1961, p. 133).

# References

This list is intended to include all, but only, those works mentioned in the text. For works first published in earlier centuries and for some others the dates given in the text are those of first publication, though the page references are to the more recent editions. The more usual alternative practice both irritates some and encourages anachronistic misconceptions in others! Both dates are given in the reference list, the date of the original publication in square brackets and the date of the edition used in round parentheses.

Anderson, D. (ed.) (1984) *The Kindness that Kills* (London: SPCK).

Arblaster, A. (1970) 'Education and Ideology', in D. Rubinstein and C. Stoneman (eds) *Education for Democracy* (Harmondsworth: Penguin).

Ardal, P. S. (1966) *Passion and Value in Hume's Treatise* (Edinburgh: Edinburgh UP).

Arnauld, A. [1662] (1964) *The Art of Thinking* (now always known as the *Port-Royal Logic*), translated by J. Dickoff and P. James (Indianapolis: Bobbs-Merrill).

Austin, J. L. (1961) *Philosophical Papers*, edited by J. O. Urmson and G. J. Warnock (Oxford: Clarendon).

Austin, J. L. (1962a) *Sense and Sensibilia*, reconstructed by G. J. Warnock (Oxford: Clarendon).

Austin, J. L. (1962b) *How to do Things with Words*, edited by J. O. Urmson (Oxford: Clarendon).

Ayer, A. J. (1946) *Language, Truth and Logic* (London: Gollancz, Second Edition).

Ayer, A. J. (1956) *The Problem of Knowledge* (London: Macmillan).

Ayer, A. J. (1980) *Hume* (Oxford: OUP).

Basson, A. H. (1958) *David Hume* (Harmondsworth: Penguin).

Beattie, J. (1770) *An Essay on the Nature and Immutability of Truth* (London).

Beauchamp, T. L. and Rosenberg, A. (1981) *Hume and the Problem of Causation* (New York and Oxford: OUP).

Bentham, J. [1776] (1948) *A Fragment on Government*, edited by W. Harrison (Oxford: Blackwell).

Berger, P. L. and Luckmann, T. (1971) *The Social Construction of Reality* (Harmondsworth: Penguin).

Berkeley, G. [1710](1901) *A Treatise concerning the Principles of Human Knowledge*, in *The Works of George Berkeley*, edited by A. C. Fraser (Oxford: Clarendon), vol. I.

Berkeley, G. [1732] *Alciphron; or, the Minute Philosopher* in the same.

Black, M. (1958) 'Making Something Happen', in S. Hook (ed.) *Determinism and Freedom in the Age of Modern Science* (New York: NYUP); also reprinted in M. Black, *Models and Metaphors* (Ithaca, New York: Cornell UP, 1962).

Bongie, L. L. (1965) *David Hume, Prophet of the Counter-Revolution* (Oxford: Clarendon).

Bradley, F. H. [1874](1935) *The Presuppositions of Critical History*. This pamphlet is most easily found reprinted in vol. I of the *Collected Essays* (Oxford: Clarendon).

Broad, C. D. (1930) *Five Types of Ethical Theory* (London: Kegan Paul).

Brownsey, P. F. (1978) 'Hume and the Social Contract', in the *Philosophical Quarterly*.

Burtt, E. A. (1932) *Metaphysical Foundations of Modern Science* (London: Kegan Paul, Trench, Trubner).

Butler, J. [1726](1896) *Fifteen Sermons*, in *Butler's Works*, edited by W. E. Gladstone (Oxford: Clarendon).

Butler, J. [1736](1896) *The Analogy of Religion*, in the same.

Capaldi, N. (1975) *David Hume, the Newtonian Philosopher* (Boston: Twayne).

Carroll, L. [1865](1939) *Alice's Adventures in Wonderland*, in *The Complete Works of Lewis Carroll* (London: Nonsuch).

Carroll, L. [1872] *Through the Looking Glass*, in the same.

Chappell, V. C. (ed.)(1966) *Hume: a Collection of Critical Essays* (GardenCity, NY: Doubleday).

Cicero, M. T. (1959) *de Officiis*, translated by W. Miller (London: Heinemann, and Cambridge, Mass.: Harvard UP).

Cicero, M. T., (1967) *Academica*, translated by H. Rackham (London: Heinemann and Cambridge, Mass.: Harvard UP).

Cicero, M. T. (1967) *de Natura Deorum*, translated by H. Rackham (London: Heinemann, and Cambridge, Mass.: Harvard UP).

Clarke, S. (1738) *Works* (London: Knapton).

Coleman, A. and others (1985) *Utopia on Trial: Vision and Reality in Planned Housing* (London: Shipman).

Collingwood, R. G. (1946) *The Idea of History* (Oxford: Clarendon).

Cottingham, J. G. (1984) *Rationalism* (London: Paladin).

Cowley, F. (1968) *A Critique of British Empiricism* (London: Macmillan, and New York: St Martins)

Denzinger, H. (1953) *Enchiridion Symbolorum* (Freiburg im Breisgau: Herder, Twenty-Ninth Revised Edition).

Descartes, R. [1637](1911) *A Discourse on the Method*, in vol. I of *The Philosophical Works of Descartes*, translated by E. S. Haldane and G. R. T. Ross (Cambridge: CUP).

Descartes, R. [1642](1911) *Meditations on First Philosophy*, in the same.

Descartes, R. [1644](1911) *The Principles of Philosophy*, in the same.

Ferguson, A. [1767] (1966) *An Essay on the History of Civil Society*, edited by D. Forbes (Edinburgh: Edinburgh UP).

Flew, A. G. N. (1950) ' "Selves" ', in *Mind*.

Flew, A. G. N. (1951) 'Locke and the Problem of Personal Identity', *Philosophy*; reprinted in revised versions in C. B. Martin and D. M. Armstrong (eds) *Locke and Berkeley* (New York: Doubleday, 1968) and B. Brody (ed.) *Readings in the Philosophy of Religion* (Englewood Cliffs, NJ: Prentice Hall, 1974), also in Flew, 1976a.

Flew A. G. N. (1953) *A New Approach to Psychical Research* (London: C. A. Watts).

Flew, A. G. N. (1954) 'Could an Effect Precede its Cause?' *Proceedings of the Aristotelian Society*, supp. vol. XXVIII.

Flew, A. G. N. (1961) *Hume's Philosophy of Belief* (London: Routledge and Kegan Paul, and New York: Humanities).

Flew, A. G. N. (ed.) (1964) *Body, Mind and Death* (New York: Collier-Macmillan).

Flew, A. G. N. (1966) *God and Philosophy* (London: Hutchinson); reissued in 1984 as *God: A Critical Enquiry* by Open Court of La Salle, Illinois.

Flew, A. G. N. (1968) 'Infinite Divisibility in Hume's *Treatise*', in *Rivista Critica di Storia della Filosofia* for 1967, Fasc. IV; reprinted, with some revisions, in Livingston, 1976.

Flew, A. G. N. (1971) *An Introduction to Western Philosophy* (London: Thames and Hudson, and Indianapolis: Bobbs-Merrill).

Flew, A. G. N. (1973) 'Must Morality Pay? or, What Socrates Should have said to Thrasymachus', in C. L. Carter (ed.) *Skepticism and Moral Principles* (Evanston, Ill., New UP).

Flew, A. G. N. (1974) 'Was Berkeley a Precursor of Wittgenstein?', in W. B. Todd (ed.) *Hume and the Enlightenment* (Edinburgh: Edinburgh UP).

Flew, A. G. N. (1975) *Thinking about Thinking* (London: Fontana).

Flew, A. G. N. (1976a) *The Presumption of Atheism* (London: Elek/Pemberton); reissued in 1984 as *God, Freedom and Immortality* by Prometheus of Buffalo, NY.

Flew, A. G. N. (1976b) *Sociology, Equality and Education* (London: Macmillan).

Flew, A. G. N. (1978a) *A Rational Animal* (Oxford: Clarendon).

Flew, A. G. N. (1978b) 'Inconsistency within a "Reconciling Project" ', *Hume Studies*, IV.

Flew, A. G. N. (1980) 'Parapsychology: Science or Pseudo-Science?', in M. Hanen, M. J. Osler, and R. G. Weyant (eds) *Science, Pseudoscience and Society* (Waterloo, Ontario: Wilfrid Laurier UP); reprinted in the

*Pacific Philosophical Quarterly* for 1980 and in P. Grim (ed.) *The Occult, Science and Philosophy* (Albany NY: SUNY Press, 1982). Compare also Flew, 1986.

Flew, A. G. N. (1981) *The Politics of Procrustes* (London: Temple Smith, and Buffalo: Prometheus).

Flew, A. G. N. (1982) 'A Strong Programme for the Sociology of Belief', *Inquiry* (Oslo).

Flew, A. G. N. (1984) *Darwinian Evolution* (London: Granada Paladin).

Flew, A. G. N. (1985) *Thinking about Social Thinking* (Oxford: Blackwell).

Flew, A. G. N. (1986) 'Analyzing the Concepts of Parapsychology', in A. G. N. Flew (ed.) *Readings in the Philosophy of Parapsychology* (Buffalo: Prometheus).

Fogelin, R. J. (1985) *Hume's Skepticism in the Treatise of Human Nature* (London: Routledge and Kegan Paul).

Gaskin, J. C. A. (1978) *Hume's Philosophy of Religion* (London: Macmillan).

Green, T. H. and Grose, T. H. (eds) (1874-5) *The Philosophical Works of David Hume* (London: Longmans Green).

Greig, J. Y. T. (ed.)(1932) *The Letters of David Hume* (Oxford: Clarendon).

Hall, T. H. (1984) *The Enigma of Daniel Home* (Buffalo: Prometheus).

Hare, R. M. (1952) *The Language of Morals* (Oxford: Clarendon).

Harrison, J. (1976) *Hume's Moral Epistemology* (Oxford: Clarendon).

Hayek, F. A. (1967) *Studies in Philosophy, Politics and Economics* (London: Routledge and Kegan Paul).

Hayek, F. A. (1978) *New Studies in Philosophy, Politics, Economics and the History of Ideas* (London: Routledge and Kegan Paul).

Hegel, G. W. F. [1807](1967) *The Phenomenology of Mind*, translated by J. B. Baillie (New York: Harper and Row).

Hegel, G. W. F. [1812-6](1929) *Science of Logic*, translated by W. H. Johnston and L. G. Struthers (London: Allen and Unwin).

Hobbes, T. [1640](1839) *Human Nature*, in *The English Works of Thomas Hobbes*, edited by Sir William Molesworth (London). Reprinted Oxford 1961.

Hudson, W. D. (ed.)(1969) *The Is/Ought Question* (London: Macmillan).

Hume, D. [1739-40](1978) *A Treatise of Human Nature*, edited by L. A. Selby-Bigge, revised by P. Nidditch (Oxford: Clarendon, Second Edition).

Hume, D. [1740](1978) *An Abstract of a Treatise of Human Nature*, in the same.

Hume, D. [1741-77](1985) *Essays Moral Political and Literary*, edited by E. F. Miller (Indianapolis: Liberty Classics).

Hume, D. [1748](1975) *An Enquiry concerning Human Understanding*, in *Enquiries . . . by David Hume*, edited by L. A. Selby-Bigge, revised by P. Nidditch (Oxford: Clarendon, Third Edition).

Hume, D. [1751](1975) *An Enquiry concerning the Principles of Morals*, in the same.

180     *References*

Hume, D. [1752] *Political Discourses*, in Hume [1741-77](1985).

Hume, D. [1754-62](1983-5) *The History of England from the Invasion of Julius Caesar to The Revolution of 1688*, edited by W. F. Todd (Indianapolis: Liberty Classics).

Hume, D. [1757](1956) *The Natural History of Religion*, edited by H. E. Root (London: A. and C. Black).

Hume, D. [1779](1947) *Dialogues concerning Natural Religion*, edited by N. Kemp Smith (Edinburgh: Nelson, Second Edition).

Jones, P. (1976) 'Strains in Hume and Wittgenstein', in D. Livingston (ed.) *Hume: A Re-Evaluation* (New York: Fordham UP).

Jones, P. (1982) *Hume's Sentiments* (Edinburgh: Edinburgh UP).

Kant, I. [1781](1929) *A Critique of Pure Reason*, the text of the 1787 Second Edition translated by N. Kemp Smith (London: Macmillan).

Kant, I. [1783](1953) *Prolegomena to any Future Metaphysics*, translated by P. G. Lucas (Manchester: Manchester UP).

Kant, I. [1785](1949) *Groundwork of the Metaphysic of Morals*, translated by H. J. Paton as *The Moral Law* (London: Hutchinson).

Kemp Smith, N. (1941) *The Philosophy of David Hume* (London: Macmillan).

Klibansky, R. and Mossner, E. C. (1954) *New Letters of David Hume* (Oxford: Clarendon).

Keuhn, M. (1979) 'A Prussian Hume and a Scottish Kant', in D. F. Norton, N. Capaldi and W. L. Robinson (eds) *Mcgill Hume Studies* (San Diego: Austin Hill).

Kuehn, M. (1983) 'Kant's Conception of "Hume's Problem"' *Journal of the History of Philosophy*.

Laird, J. (1932) *Hume's Philosophy of Human Nature* (London: Methuen).

Lewis, H. D. (1959) *Our Experience of God* (London: Allen and Unwin).

Livingston, D. (ed.) (1976) *Hume: A Reevaluation* (New York: Fordham UP).

Livingston, D. (1984) *Hume's Philosophy of Common Life* (Chicago: Chicago UP).

Locke, J. [1690a](1975) *An Essay concerning Human Understanding*, edited by P. H. Nidditch (Oxford: Clarendon).

Locke, J. [1690b](1960) *Two Treatises of Civil Government*, edited by P. Laslett (Cambridge: CUP).

Mackie, J. L. (1974) *The Cement of the Universe* (Oxford: Clarendon).

Mackie, J. L. (1980) *Hume's Moral Theory* (London: Routledge and Kegan Paul).

MacNabb, D. G. C. and Khamara, E. J. 'Hume and his Predecessors on the Causal Maxim', in Morice, 1977, pp. 146-55.

Marx, K. and Engels, F. [1848](1967) *The Communist Manifesto*, translated by Samuel Moore and edited by A. J. P. Taylor (Harmondsworth: Penguin).

Marx, K. [1867](1961-2) *Capital*, translated by S. Moore and E. Aveling (London: Lawrence and Wishart).

Mill, J. S. [1843](1865) *A System of Logic, Ratiocinative and Inductive* (London: Longmans Green), Sixth Edition.

Mill, J. S. [1861](1910) *Utilitarianism*, edited by A. D. Lindsay (London: Dent, and New York: Dutton).

Moore, G. E. (1903) *Principia Ethica* (Cambridge: CUP).

Morice, G. P. (ed.)(1977) *David Hume: Bicentenary Papers* (Edinburgh: Edinburgh UP).

Mossner, E. C. (1954) *The Life of David Hume* (Edinburgh: Nelson).

Mossner, E. C. (1977) 'Hume and the Legacy of the *Dialogues*, in Morice, 1977.

Murray, C. (1984) *Losing Ground: American Social Policy 1950-1980* (New York: Basic).

Newton, I. [1686](1962) *Principia Mathematica Philosophiae Naturalis*, translated by A. Motte, revised and edited by F. Cajon (Berkeley and Los Angeles: California UP).

Newton, I. [1704](1952) *Opticks*, edited by I. B. Cohen (New York: Dover).

Noxon, J. (1973) *Hume's Philosophical Development* (Oxford: Clarendon).

Okie, L. (1985) 'Ideology and Partiality in David Hume's *History of England*', *Hume Studies*.

Passmore, J. A. (1952) *Hume's Intentions* (Cambridge: CUP).

Penelhum, T. (1955) 'Hume on Personal Identity', *Philosophical Review*.

Penelhum, T. (1960) 'Divine Necessity', *Mind*.

Penelhum, T. (1975) *Hume* (London: Macmillan).

Plato (1963) *The Republic*, translated by P. Shorey (London: Heinemann, Cambridge, Mass.: Harvard UP).

Popkin, R. H. (1964) *The History of Scepticism from Erasmus to Descartes* (Assen: van Gorcum).

Popper, K. R. [1934](1959) *The Logic of Scientific Discovery* (London: Hutchinson).

Popper, K. R. [1945](1956) *The Open Society and its Enemies* (London: Routledge and Kegan Paul), Fifth Edition.

Popper, K. R. (1957) *The Poverty of Historicism* (London: Routledge and Kegan Paul).

Popper, K. R. (1963) *Conjectures and Refutations* (London: Routledge and Kegan Paul).

Popper, K. R. [1972](1979) *Objective Knowledge* (Oxford: Clarendon, Revised Edition).

Popper, K. R. (1982) *The Open Universe: An Argument for Indeterminism* (London: Hutchinson).

Popper, K. R. and Eccles, J. C. (1977), *The Self and Its Brain* (Berlin, New York and London: Springer International).

Price, H. H. (1932) *Perception* (London: Methuen).

Price, H. H. (1940a) *Hume's Theory of the External World* (Oxford: Clarendon).

Price, H. H. (1940b) 'The Permanent Significance of Hume's Philosophy',

*Philosophy*; reprinted in A. Sesonske and N. Fleming (eds) *Human Understanding: Studies in the Philosophy of David Hume* (Belmont, Calif: Wadsworth, 1965).

Prichard, H. A. (1949) *Moral Obligation* (Oxford: Clarendon).

Quine, W. V. O. (1963) 'Two Dogmas of Empiricism', in his *From a Logical Point of View* (New York: Harper, Second Edition).

Rae, J. (1895) *A Life of Adam Smith* (London).

Rawls, J. (1971) *A Theory of Justice* (Cambridge, Mass.: Harvard UP, and Oxford: Clarendon, 1972).

Robertson, W. (1890) *The Works of William Robertson* (Edinburgh).

Robinson, J. A. (1962) 'Hume's Two Definitions of "Cause"', *Philosophical Quarterly;* reprinted in Chappell, 1966.

Rotwein, E. (1953) *Hume: Writings on Economics* (Madison: Wisconsin University Press).

Rousseau, J-J [1762](1958) *The Social Contract and Discourses*, edited by G. D. H. Cole (London: Dent, and New York: Dutton).

Ruse, M. (1986) *Taking Darwin Seriously: A Naturalistic Approach to Philosophy* (Oxford: Blackwell).

Russell, P. (1985) 'Hume's *Treatise* and Hobbes' *Elements of Law*', *Journal of the History of Ideas*.

Ryle, G. (1949) *The Concept of Mind* (London: Hutchinson).

Skinner, B. F. (1948) *Walden Two* (New York: Macmillan).

Skinner, B. F. (1953) *Science and Human Behavior* (New York: Macmillan).

Skinner, B. F. (1971) *Beyond Freedom and Dignity* (New York: Knopf, and London: Cape, 1972).

Sloan, P. (ed.)(1938) *John Cornford: A Memoir* (London: Cape).

Smith, A. [1776](1976) *An Inquiry into the Nature and Causes of the Wealth of Nations*, edited by R. H. Campbell and A. S. Skinner (Oxford: Clarendon).

Stephen, L. [1876] *History of English Thought in the Eighteenth Century* (London: Murray) The third edition of 1902 was in 1949 reprinted by Peter Smith of New York.

Stout, G. F. (1950) 'Mechanical and Teleological Causality', *Proceedings of the Aristotelian Society*, supp. vol. XXIV.

Stove, D. (1973) *Probability and Hume's Inductive Scepticism* (Oxford: Clarendon).

Stove, D. (1982) *Popper and After: Four Modern Irrationalists* (Oxford: Pergamon).

Stroud, B. (1977) *Hume* (London: Routledge and Kegan Paul).

Valla, L. *Dialogue on Freewill*, translated by C. E. Trinkhaus, in E. Cassirer, P. O. Cristeller and J. H. Randall (eds) *The Renaissance Philosophy of Man* (Chicago: Chicago UP).

Voltaire, F. M. A. (1883-7) *Oeuvres Complètes* (Paris).

Wesley, J. ]1827](1906-16) *The Journals of John Wesley*, edited by N. Curnock (London: Epworth).

Wittgenstein, L. [1921](1922) *Tractatus Logico-Philosophicus*, translated by C. K. Ogden (London: Kegan Paul, Trench, Trubner).

Wittgenstein, L. (1953) *Philosophical Investigations*, translated by G. E. M. Anscombe (Oxford: Blackwell).

Wright, J. P. (1983) *The Sceptical Realism of David Hume* (Manchester: Manchester UP).

# Index of Names

# Index of Notions

*Note*: Since this index is intended as a tool for students, especially for those revising, it aims to list only places where ideas are defined or discussed rather than used or merely mentioned.